SEEKING A GENTLE & QUIET SPIRIT

in a Harsh and Noisy World

Amber Albee Swenson

NORTHWESTERN PUBLISHING HOUSE
Milwaukee, Wisconsin

Design: Lynda Williams
Cover: Image used under license from iStock
Illustration: by KatyaDanilova at VectorStock.com

Northwestern Publishing House
N16W23379 Stone Ridge Dr., Waukesha WI 53188-1108
www.nph.net
© 2024 by Northwestern Publishing House
Published 2024
Printed in the United States of America
ISBN 978-0-8100-3206-4
ISBN 978-0-8100-3207-1 (e-book)

24 25 26 27 28 29 30 31 32 33   10 9 8 7 6 5 4 3 2 1

Preface

First Peter chapter 3 might not be listed as your favorite chapter of the Bible. In fact, it might be a chapter you avoid. It starts, "Wives, in the same way submit ..."

Hello? Are you still there?

In the middle of the paragraph, two verses catch my attention. They say, "Your beauty should not come from outward adornment, such as elaborate hairstyles and the wearing of gold jewelry or fine clothes. Rather, it should be that of your inner self, the unfading beauty of a gentle and quiet spirit, which is of great worth in God's sight" (1 Peter 3:3,4).

Um ...

That is as counterculture as it gets. Your beauty shouldn't come from hair, clothes, or jewelry? If Peter had added makeup, it would be all over. What's left?

What's left is what is important to God. In fact, of great worth to God. To my knowledge those words don't appear anywhere else in the Bible. This is of great worth in God's sight.

What is?

"The unfading beauty of a gentle and quiet spirit."

If that's the case, I need to figure out what that means. I've watched YouTube videos to put on makeup and to curl my hair. How do I learn to have a gentle and quiet spirit?

Come with me, and we'll find out together.

TABLE OF CONTENTS

CHAPTER 1

A Gentle and Quiet Spirit Comes From Time in the Word and Prayer

Pursue a relationship with God

Read 1 Timothy 6:6-12.

If you've ever known a woman with a gentle and quiet spirit, you don't forget her. She is not easily flustered. She doesn't make something more of an issue than it is. She knows when to say what needs to be said and says it in a way that makes everyone think, without destroying anyone in the process. She doesn't seek the spotlight, but when attention comes her way, she uses it to shine a light on God's glory. She exhibits calm, dignity, and strength. A gentle and quiet spirit will impact everyone in a woman's life. If that isn't reason enough to want these traits, here's the best reason: It's God's desire.

The apostle Peter tells women in 1 Peter 3:3,4, "Your beauty should not come from outward adornment, such as elaborate hairstyles and the wearing of gold jewelry or fine clothes. Rather, it should be that of your inner self, the unfading beauty of a gentle and quiet spirit, which is of great worth in God's sight." A gentle and quiet spirit is of great worth to God. I can't think of a better reason to pursue anything.

To pursue is "to seek to attain over a long period; and to continue along a path in order to someday possess something." Acquiring a gentle and quiet spirit is a lifelong pursuit because it requires a daily battle against our sinful nature. Our sinful nature wants its own way. It announces others' shortcomings and squashes voices of dissent. It pushes slowpokes to the side with no concern for their feelings or opinions.

Squelching the sinful nature is, as Martin Luther said, drowning our sinful nature (old Adam) by "daily contrition and repentance" in order that a "new person should daily arise to live . . . in righteousness and purity."[1] Contrition, or sorrow for sins, needs to be refined. Spending time on Hulu, Netflix, Amazon Prime, or a popular daytime or evening drama will likely do more to ambush contrition than embrace it. Secular songs will encourage our old Adam to ignore any tinge of guilt our conscience sends. Social media will offer distraction or, at best, a meme of Scripture, a blog, or a video. And all too often that's where our pursuit ends.

Imagine a hunting dog that caught the scent of the prey and a short sniff was enough to satisfy its craving to hunt. It's unimaginable! Setters and pointers enthusiastically track their prey and zealously lead their masters to it. Retrievers can sit for hours intently watching their owners hunt and, upon command, race to bring back every downed bird. Imagine a retriever dozing during the hunt and, when called upon, trotting to retrieve only the closest bird, considering his job complete. Such a dog would be useless to his master and replaced immediately.

The apostle Paul told Timothy to pursue righteousness, godliness, faith, love, endurance, and gentleness. If we search for these things like a setter or pointer, we will find them in God's Word. And once found, they can be planted in our hearts.

Step 1 is to develop a taste for these qualities. We won't pursue what we don't want. I won't make the effort to go to the gym if I don't care about health. If I don't make keeping my house a priority, especially with four children at home, I won't keep up with the daily clutter and mess that accumulate.

Tastes can be refined. Years ago, our family eliminated corn syrup and processed food from our diet and started eating considerably more vegetables. What seemed drastic at the time is our

---

[1] Martin Luther, *Luther's Catechism* (Milwaukee: Northwestern Publishing House, 2017), p. 10.

norm now. The same will happen spiritually. As we recognize the spiritually deficient options and make different choices, we'll find secular choices less appetizing and desire the things of God more.

For further consideration/discussion:
1. Can we just be honest? Understand, I'm not trying to shame you. I'm looking in the mirror with you. How much time do you spend on media devices each day?

2. What content are you most likely to consume?

3. Again, no shame, just an honest question: Are you in the Word of God every day? If so, how long do you spend reading the Bible or listening to a Bible app? If not every day, do you read the Bible most days, some days, or not at all?

How to pursue a relationship with God

Read 2 Chronicles 15:2; Jeremiah 33:3; and James 1:5.

Some things you could chase your whole life and never get. If I worked full time for the next 20 years and put my entire paycheck in the bank, I still might not have a million dollars. If I worked out three hours every day and invested in makeup and haircuts, I still wouldn't look like a supermodel.

Pursuing God is a winning endeavor. He assures us that when we seek him, call on him, and ask him for wisdom, the answer is yes. I'm not sure we understand the immensity of this.

When I call to make a dentist appointment, sometimes I can't get in for a month. Even if I'm in pain, it's not always possible to see the dentist that day. I'd have to go through a lot of red tape to see my governor if I had an idea for running the state more efficiently. I wouldn't even attempt to see the president.

In contrast, the Creator of all things, the all-powerful God who keeps everything in motion, gives us unlimited access to his throne room, 24/7/365. And because he loves us and doesn't want us to flounder, he gave us a book that chronicles his love, assures us of his promises, guides us in righteousness, instructs us to avoid pitfalls, and gives us examples of success and failure through many generations.

Five hundred years ago, Martin Luther was working hard to get the Bible into people's hands. Today, most of us have one or more Bibles in our homes, a Bible app on our phones, and access to the Bible on our laptops. If we want to dig deeper and understand more, we have commentaries, sermons, podcasts, blogs, and even papers from professors at the seminary a click away. God has given us all we need. I heard a pastor say that most people don't reject Jesus. They just never get around to making him a priority.

Every day we are beaten down by the struggles of living in a fallen world. It's easy to lose hope and wonder how to make sense of it all. But when we open the pages of Scripture, God meets us in our disorder. His Word strengthens us and gives us comfort and hope. It reminds us of God's promises and love—a love that isn't dependent on how much we've accomplished, how we look, or how much we earn. In a world that constantly distorts the truth, God's Word offers truth from the source of truth.

Why do I neglect God's Word and prayer when it is everything I'm looking for, never fails, and is absolutely free? Too often I've scoured the internet and called my friends searching for answers they can't give. I fret and scurry and convince myself I don't have time to read the Bible or pray. How foolish to think I don't have time to go to the one who holds the answers! That's like holding a cell phone with a dead battery while standing next to a charger and power source.

People often ask where to start. When you get serious about God's Word, is it imperative to start at the beginning? What about the Old Testament laws? How can you tell what was God's design for a time but no longer applies because it's been fulfilled in Christ?

The best answer I've heard to these questions came from Pastor Mike Novotny from Time of Grace Ministry. He said when you get serious about reading the Bible, maybe the most important thing you could do is study it with another mature Christian and, if you're able, join a Bible study. Good Bible study leaders will fill in the blanks. They will research and study prior to class so they can pass along what they've learned.

I've taught women's Bible studies for years, and part of my preparation is to read the section from The People's Bible series that coincides with what I'm teaching. Sometimes my pastor, or a pastor from a different church, gives me a paper or another book on the subject so I have all the background information and commentary to teach the Word in truth and purity.

An added blessing to being part of a Bible study group is the fellowship of other Christians. It's not uncommon for people to stay after class and catch up, to share the latest about their lives and ask for prayers. They exchange phone numbers and text prayer requests. Some gather outside of class for coffee or playdates with children. Small group studies offer insight into the Word and help us grow closer to God. The participants in your Bible study can become an amazing support group for you. The greatest blessing is the one that Jesus promises in Matthew 28:20: "For where two or three gather in my name, there am I with them."

For further consideration/discussion:
   4. What obstacles and excuses keep you from reading the Bible and spending time with God in prayer?

   5. Read Mark 1:29-39. Jesus was as busy as any of us will get. Mark says, "The whole town gathered" and "Jesus healed many." Yet Jesus made time to pray. Considering who Jesus was and that he prayed, what can we take away from this?

6. Think about where and when Jesus went to pray. What can we learn about prayer from this account?

Putting it into practice

Read Luke 10:38-42 and James 1:22-25.

There are two really important points to note after reading these sections of Scripture. First, a good many of us are doers. We jump into action the minute there is something to do. Our volunteer résumé is long. But Jesus knew what so many of us forget. If our volunteer activity comes at the expense of time in the Word, we are missing out. We'll miss out on the gentle and quiet spirit he would give us. Then we end up serving like Martha: stressed out, upset others aren't helping, and complaining either out loud or in our spirit. Mary showed us the solution. It is found by spending time at Jesus' feet listening to his words.

Nothing robs me of my gentle and quiet spirit faster than neglecting time with the Lord. While a concerted effort to make behavioral changes is honorable, our human nature is frail and we're prone to failure. No matter how hard I try, my sinful nature makes me fierce and loud more often than gentle and quiet.

True and lasting change happens as the gospel changes us. The gospel—that Jesus left the glory of heaven to live the righteous life we couldn't and pay our sin debt with his death and resurrection—chips away at my hard heart. As I understand the depth of God's love in calling me his child, I want to be more like him.

Most of us have witnessed or seen pictures of a little boy with his toy mower walking up and down the lawn next to his dad. The father has shown his love for his son, and because the little boy loves his father, he wants to be just like him. That's how sanctification works. As we understand and experience the depth of God's love, we want to be just like him, not to earn a place in heaven but because we see he is truth, love, goodness, and faithfulness. He is everything our hearts crave but rarely find in this sin-sick world.

As we spend time with him, we become more like him. We'll talk the way he talks and act the way he acts just because we've been with him and heard what he said.

And that brings us to the second important point: How do we read the Bible in such a way that it changes us? It is possible to be the person James was talking about. I've done it more often than I want to admit. I've put my time in and checked off the box, shutting my Bible without being sure what I just read.

I'm trying to read the Bible less and study it more. Let me explain. I used to read a chapter of the Bible each night before bed. It wasn't a bad plan. In fact, I read my Bible from front to back several times doing just that. These days I don't worry about how much I read each day. Instead I meditate on the verses, read the notes in my study Bible, and pray my way through the reading. It is easier to apply the Word and do what it says when you understand it, think about it, and pray about it.

Jesus invited many people to follow him. He offers us the same invitation. If we want a gentle and quiet spirit, the place to start is in our study of his Word. Time with Jesus will transform us just as time with Jesus transformed the disciples. The Holy Spirit, other Christians, and Christian pastors and teachers will fan the flame of faith, and the fruit of the Spirit will be a by-product.

For further consideration/discussion:

7. Read the following passages from Psalm 119 and write down the benefits we receive when we spend time in the Word and prayer.

   Psalm 119:28

   Psalm 119:36,37

   Psalm 119:49,50

   Psalm 119:104

   Psalm 119:160

   Psalm 119:165

8. There's a reason it's important to let God work in our hearts before we serve him. The way we serve matters. Read these passages and write down what they teach us about how we ought to serve.

   Luke 9:62

   Luke 17:7-10

   Romans 12:11

9. Now read Luke 12:47,48. What are we forgetting when we're feeling overwhelmed by what we have to do or if we're thinking others aren't doing enough?

10. If you're a Martha by nature, you will need an action plan to keep you from slipping into serving with an attitude. When we're irritated and overwhelmed, what can we do to mentally switch gears so we serve willingly and joyfully?

Key takeaways:

 ✝ God says a gentle and quiet spirit is of great worth to him. I want to pursue anything God says is of great worth!

 ✝ If we aren't in the Word, we can't know God's will and God's ways. If we're not in the Word, the ways of the world are most likely our norm.

 ✝ God is not like our earthly leaders. He's available to us and wants to give his wisdom to us. He wants to replace our anxiety, disorder, and frustration with a gentle and quiet spirit.

 ✝ God would have us prioritize a relationship with him, even above serving.

✝ Serving with the wrong attitude doesn't glorify God. It's best for us to get our attitudes under control and then go back to serving.

✝ Service that glorifies God is done willingly, joyfully, and with the strength God provides.

Prayer to close:

Almighty Father, forgive us for the times we've been women of the world instead of women of the Word. Work in our hearts and minds. Create in us a hunger for your Word. Help us to learn your ways so we can teach others and glorify you. In Jesus' name. Amen.

CHAPTER 2
Weathering Storms

When you don't see or feel God in the storm

Read Mark 4:35-41.

Sudden and violent storms were nothing unusual on the Sea of Galilee. This storm was different. These professional fishermen were shaken to the core. Anyone who has been in a violent storm knows the terror. Against an ominous sky, howling wind, torrential rain, or enormous waves, we become aware of how small we really are. With the waves overtaking the boat, the disciples were convinced they were not going to survive the storm.

How many close calls have you had? Have you been on a plane bouncing with turbulence or in a car struggling to stay on the road? Have you hunkered down in your basement as the wind howled above you?

Maybe your storm had nothing to do with weather. Illness ravaged you or a friend or relative. Depression rattled a loved one. The effects of old age took a toll. Sometimes we are spared the accident. Sometimes we experience the accident and the life-changing ramifications of it. Sometimes, like the disciples, we ask, "God, where are you?"

Storms often blindside us. If we knew they were coming and had time to prepare physically and emotionally, maybe we'd know how to react. But too often we're suddenly in the middle of a situation, surrounded by circumstances way bigger than us. And just like the disciples who accused Jesus of not caring, it often seems like God is painfully silent when we need him most.

Jesus was there the whole time. The disciples didn't wake him until they were convinced they were going to drown. But he hadn't abandoned the boat or them. God is with us in our storms too. Satan wants us to think that no one has ever experienced what we're going through and that if God loved us, he would shield us from hard times. But throughout Scripture, God reminds his people that just isn't the case.

We live in a sinful world. As long as we are alive, we will experience the consequences of sin. In the first chapter of Job, God permits trying times to come into Job's life. While in the storm, we need to remember that God is allowing us to go through whatever we are going through. Even if we are taken off guard by the storm, God is not.

Sometimes the storms are to strengthen our faith. God used Moses to bring the Israelites out of slavery in Egypt. They had to cross a desert to get to the Promised Land. God provided food and water, protected them from harm, and made sure their clothes and shoes didn't wear out. He met every need as it arose.

Sometimes hardship comes to test our commitment to God. God asked Abraham to sacrifice his only son. God didn't want Isaac dead. He was testing Abraham's faith by asking him to give up the one thing he had always wanted and had waited so long to have.

Sometimes God uses hardship to turn us back to him. Throughout the book of Judges, the Israelites fell into sin, and God allowed them to be overtaken by a nearby nation. Eventually, they called out to God, and he delivered them.

Sometimes God allows hardship into our lives because his plan takes us in a different direction than we would otherwise go. God allowed Joseph to be sold into slavery and taken to Egypt. In Egypt, God used Joseph to work with Pharaoh to prepare for the famine that was going to come, saving the lives of the Egyptians and Joseph's family as well.

Sometimes God puts us in the middle of the chaos to act on behalf of his people. Esther was a young, beautiful Jewish woman who was chosen to be queen to a heathen king. God put her in a position to have sway with the king so that she might save her people from annihilation.

Still other times trouble comes as a consequence of our own actions. God sent the Israelites to Babylon as slaves to call them to repentance for their idolatry. Separation from their homeland was terrible, but not as terrible as the separation from God caused by their idolatry. God often uses the storms in our lives to draw us closer to himself.

When the disciples concluded they were about to die, they finally went to Jesus. In their fear, they accused him of not caring about their situation. If we're not careful, our prayers can become filled with accusations too: *Why would you let this happen? I thought you loved me. Do you even see me, or are you blind to this situation?*

Scripture assures us that God loves us and cares about our well-being. Satan wants us to doubt God's love, but the Bible shows us that this is a lie. It's amazing that God, who created and sustains the universe, allows us to come to him at any time and with any problem. He invites us to cast our anxieties on him and receive the answers only he can give (1 Peter 5:7). We can fumble our way through the storms while continuing to sink like the disciples on the boat, or we can go to Jesus with our struggles and trust him to calm the waves.

Just a word from Jesus brought calm to the disciples on the boat. God is bigger than our storms too. When we're feeling overwhelmed, the temptation is to think the situation is somehow bigger than God. We could blame him for our troubles. Far better to know that God is in the storm with us and knows exactly what's going on, even when we can't see it.

For further consideration/discussion:

1. Often, we don't see the blessings the storm produces until months or years later when we look back and see God's hand. How does this help us if we're in a storm now?

2. Knowing our storms have purpose changes our view of them. How so?

3. We find peace when we realize we don't have to fix anyone's storms, and most of the time, we can't. Sometimes we just have to be a good friend. What can you do to comfort someone struggling now?

Thinking of others during our storms

Read Daniel 1:8-16; 2:14-16.

If there's one group of people I'd like to emulate in the impossible situations of life, it's Daniel and his friends. These new recruits to Nebuchadnezzar's service were in a predicament. As Jews they only ate certain meats that had been prepared according to their law. But when they were forced from their homeland and into Nebuchadnezzar's service, they were expected to eat things they never would have eaten in their homeland. Not only were the meats not prepared according to the requirements of their law, but often the meat and wine were consumed as an act of worship to one of Babylon's many gods. They had to make a choice. They could fit in and expect God to understand, or they could refuse to defile themselves even if it came at a cost.

Even as a young man, Daniel didn't shy away from conflict. Rather, with wisdom (insight as to right living) and tact (a sensitivity to tone and word choice when dealing with difficult topics), Daniel approached someone in a position to help him. He asked the official for permission to eat the way he was used to eating. Though the official sympathized with Daniel, he feared the king. If Daniel and his friends didn't eat the meat and ended up looking sickly, the king would have the official's head. Daniel showed sympathy for the man's position and respect for his life. He suggested a trial period to make sure they still appeared healthy if they weren't eating the meat and drinking the wine.

Daniel wasn't so absorbed in his situation that he couldn't see the struggles of another man. He also didn't see the official as merely a means to get his way. He respected the official's concerns. He realized what he was asking could implicate the official's life.

Daniel's sensitivity to another person goes against our self-centered, self-serving sinful nature. When the waves are swirling around us and swamping the boat, it is not easy to remember that others are also in a storm. Sometimes we don't know what others are going through. It's easy to assume that if they aren't complaining, they must be enjoying smooth sailing. We should never assume all is well with other people just because we haven't heard about an issue. Perhaps it's more accurate to assume everyone we know is in a battle whether we know about it or not. To do so, even while our storm is raging, is evidence of God working in our lives.

From the cross, Jesus gave his mother into the apostle John's care. He looked beyond himself, while enduring excruciating pain, to see the needs of another. It will take Christ in us to do the same. And that only happens when we go to the Word day after day to drown our sinful nature and awaken our new self. The apostle Paul says this in Ephesians 4:22-24: "You were taught, with regard to your former way of life, to put off your old self, which is being corrupted by its deceitful desires; to be made new in the attitude of your minds; and to put on the new self, created to be like God in true righteousness and holiness."

I have a friend who has suffered through five grueling years of cancer treatments. Every time I step in to help, she suggests I have too much on my plate to be helping her. I have to assure her that I want to help and my plate is just fine. Her concern for me and my family has made an indelible impact on me. I want to be like Daniel and like this friend. Even during my difficult times, I want to be aware of the struggles others face.

A few years after Daniel arrived in Babylon, he found himself face-to-face with an executioner. Though Daniel was in a program for the elite from countries across the empire, he didn't treat the executioner as less than himself. He merely asked why the king ordered his execution. In our impossible situations, it can be hard to remain calm, and yet Daniel shows us that tact will often take us further than demeaning or demanding talk. I struggle to remain calm and choose kind words when dealing with customer service in non-life-threatening matters. Controlling our words and keeping our emotions in check is a fruit of the Spirit. He can bestow on us the self-control to treat everyone as a beloved child of God. In the whole scheme of things, my customer service struggles are minor. What a difference it would make if we kept our tempers in check and used kind words and a gentle tone. Whether we get our way or not isn't the issue. If we have self-control, we can glorify God through our words and actions in the middle of the storm.

For further consideration/discussion:

4. What is in our hearts when we make demands?

5. Daniel didn't waste time talking to the other recruits to see if they had dietary restrictions. What is the lesson and application for us in our impossible situations?

6. Another thing we don't see Daniel doing is wondering how he got in this predicament and whose fault it was. Why are those things not worth our time and energy?

Seeing God in the storm

Read Ruth 1:19-22 and Daniel 3:13-18.

In the book of Ruth, we are introduced to Naomi, her two sons, and her husband, Elimelech. They left Israel during a famine and took refuge in Moab. During their time in Moab, the two sons married. Eventually, Elimelech and both sons died, and Naomi and one daughter-in-law returned to Bethlehem.

Like the disciples during the storm, Naomi fell into a common temptation. When things aren't going our way, troubles overtake us, or God doesn't answer our prayers the way we hoped, it's easy to think God has forsaken us.

Ruth 1:22 may seem to contain a trivial detail: The women arrived in Israel as the barley harvest began. If we were to read on, in Ruth, we would see God's unmistakable providence. The barley harvest provided a means of food for the women and ultimately was the vehicle God used to bring Boaz and Ruth together. Often, we see the circumstances without seeing God working in, through, and around the circumstances.

I've learned while in the storm to simply pray, "Lord, I know you are in this boat. If you aren't going to calm the waves or silence the wind, then calm my fears and silence my worries." During times of stress, I like to sing and pray Psalm 51:10-12: "Create in me a pure heart, O God, and renew a steadfast spirit within me. Do not cast me from your presence or take your Holy Spirit from me. Restore to me the joy of your salvation and grant me a willing spirit, to sustain me."

Shadrach, Meshach, and Abednego teach us an important lesson about weathering the storm quietly. They did not presume to know how or if God was going to act on their behalf. Even if he didn't, they would go to their deaths glorifying him with their actions. It's common to give glory to God if he answers our prayers the way we hoped he would. Shadrach, Meshach, and Abednego teach us not to limit God that way. God still would have been good even if he had taken these men home through the fire. God was good when John the Baptist was beheaded (Matthew 14) and when Stephen was stoned to death (Acts 7:54-60). How can we say that? Stephen saw heaven opening to receive him. John the Baptist too went from life in a dungeon to eternal glory the moment his life ended on earth. Even if we get the worst-case scenario on earth, God provided for us eternally by sending Jesus to pay for our sins.

The apostle Paul suggests we "rejoice always, pray continually, give thanks in all circumstances; for this is God's will for you in Christ Jesus" (1 Thessalonians 5:16-18). Praising and thanking God shouldn't be limited to the times he answers our prayers the way we hoped he would. Why? Because we can't always see his purposes and plans. We can't always recognize the way he is working all things for our good. Good Friday was a terrible day for the disciples. It wasn't until after Jesus rose from the dead and explained the Scriptures to the men on the road to Emmaus that the disciples started to understand that Jesus' death had purpose and meaning.

How we act during the storms of life need not be dependent on whether or not we see God in the storms. Consider this account from Acts 16:16-25:

> Once when we were going to the place of prayer, we were met by a female slave who had a spirit by which she predicted the future. She earned a great deal of money for her owners by fortune-telling. She followed Paul and the rest of us, shouting, "These men are servants of the Most High God, who are telling you the way to be saved." She kept this up for many days. Finally Paul became so annoyed that he turned around and said to the spirit, "In the name of Jesus Christ I command you to come out of her!" At that moment the spirit left her.
>
> When her owners realized that their hope of making money was gone, they seized Paul and Silas and dragged them into the marketplace to face the authorities. They brought them before the magistrates and said, "These men are Jews, and are throwing our city into an uproar by advocating customs unlawful for us Romans to accept or practice."
>
> The crowd joined in the attack against Paul and Silas, and the magistrates ordered them to be stripped and

beaten with rods. After they had been severely flogged, they were thrown into prison, and the jailer was commanded to guard them carefully. When he received these orders, he put them in the inner cell and fastened their feet in the stocks.

About midnight Paul and Silas were praying and singing hymns to God, and the other prisoners were listening to them.

Paul and Silas were seized, dragged, stripped, and beaten with rods. They were "severely flogged," thrown into prison, and put in stocks. If we don't slow down while reading this, we might miss how terrible the whole experience was. I have never been publicly seized, stripped, and flogged. These days, stocks are picture opportunities at tourist sites, but there was a time when they were used to restrain and restrict prisoners. Having your feet in stocks meant you were stuck in one position with limited movement. That might not seem bad at first, but it would be more difficult with each passing hour.

This was the physical state of Paul and Silas at midnight as they were singing hymns to God. Their worship attracted the attention of the other prisoners. Paul and Silas were treated unjustly. They were Roman citizens who were beaten and imprisoned without the benefit of a trial. They might have complained or demanded immediate release. Instead, they immersed themselves in worship and prayer, glorifying God in the middle of the storm even when they didn't know the outcome.

It seems impossible, doesn't it? To worship and praise in the most difficult moments seems to ask more of a mere mortal than what's possible. We are only able to do this when we trust God completely, when we know beyond a shadow of a doubt that God has a good and gracious plan and purpose for us, even if we don't see or understand it. And when we fall short, as I do so often, it's best to admit it, repent, and move on. God doesn't base his love on our performances but on his grace and forgiveness. He has a plan and a purpose for our lives whether or not we acknowledge it. He walks beside us even when we stagger.

Storms are unique opportunities to show an unbelieving world what it is to walk with God. When we choose to show unwavering trust rather than complain or blame God, we show the world that God is worthy of our worship and trust regardless of our circumstances.

For further consideration/discussion:

7. What reminders and promises can we keep in front of us to help us weather the storms well?

8. Like Naomi, we often can't see the simple but profound ways God is working in our lives. How can we start to see God's providence instead of just the circumstances?

9. Stephen was stoned to death, and John the Baptist was beheaded. From a worldly perspective, this is a worst-case scenario. How can we glorify God while weathering storms when the worst happens?

Key takeaways:

† In the Word, God reminds us that we are his people, and he is concerned with our well-being.

† So often it seems God either isn't aware of or doesn't care about the situation. We can be certain neither is true.

✝ Using wisdom and tact in our conversations in the middle of storms is a beautiful way to honor God regardless of the outcome.

✝ Praying brings God into the situation. Not only can he calm our fears, but he also can deliver us from the storm.

✝ God is good whether or not he answers our prayers the way we hope.

Prayer to close:

Holy Father, help us honor and glorify you all the days of our lives but especially during storms. In our troubles we are given a unique opportunity to honor you when many would curse you and accuse you of not caring. Help us honor you in every circumstance so that our words and actions lead others to trust you. In Jesus' name we pray. Amen.

CHAPTER 3

Remembering God's Faithfulness During Seasons of Change

Learning to face change without grumbling

Read Exodus 15:22-27.

Most of us have short memories. Our boss gives us a bonus at Christmas, but the first memo in the new year has us complaining. Our spouse gives us a compliment, but within the hour we're struggling with insecurity. God delivers us from one situation, but the next time we're in a pickle, we're frantically wondering how we're going to make it. Is it possible to stop the amnesia?

In the first ten chapters of the book of Exodus, God revealed how he delivered the people from Egypt. When Pharaoh refused to let God's people go, God brought ten plagues on the Egyptians. The Israelites experienced three of the plagues but were protected from the flies, the disease on livestock, the boils, the hail, the locusts, the darkness, and the death of the firstborn.

When Pharaoh told the Israelites to leave, they made it as far as the Red Sea before Pharaoh gathered his army to chase them. The Israelites were trapped: Pharaoh's army was behind, and the Red Sea was in front of them. The angel of God, who had been leading them, went behind the people, as did the pillar of cloud that had gone before them. God parted the Red Sea for the people to cross on dry ground. He kept the Israelites in daylight to safely cross while keeping the Egyptians in the dark to prevent them from pursuing.

Once the Israelites were safely across, God allowed the Egyptians to follow them into the sea. As they did, the wheels fell off their chariots and the walls of water fell, drowning the Egyptian army. In bringing about the plagues and allowing the Israelites to cross the Red Sea, God revealed he was almighty. He could inflict terror and disease on one group of people while protecting and providing for another. You might think, as I so often do, that if you experienced a miracle of that magnitude, your faith would never falter. I wish that were so, but a close examination of my life shows I'm no better than my Israelite ancestors.

God still provides. We have ample food in our cupboards, freezers, and pantries. Rain falls, the sun shines, and crops grow. We breathe mostly clean air, drink clean water, and have jobs to keep us in temperature-controlled houses and sleeping in soft beds. These are often overlooked examples of God's continued faithfulness.

But let's not forget the times we asked God to keep our children safe or to heal a loved one who was sick. Remember the flights that landed, the car rides that brought us safely to our destination, and the peace that our country enjoys. God's faithfulness is evident as we wake up each day to another day of grace. It's evident each time we say we're sorry and know we are forgiven.

The events in our reading in Exodus occurred less than a week after the miraculous parting of the Red Sea. The Israelites were led into the wilderness of Shur. The People's Bible explains that "it was a desolate area" with "bare limestone hills and rocky valleys through which they had to travel."[2] And then they experienced a need, not just a new mattress or a different shade of nail polish but a legitimate need. Traversing through rocky terrain without water to refresh would not make for easy travel.

Immediately, the Israelites grumbled. Before we think how ungrateful those Israelites were, consider how easy it is to do the same, especially if we focus only on what we lack and the less than ideal circumstances. Isn't that what we often do?

If we want to respond differently, then we need a different approach. The writer of Hebrews gives it to us.

---

[2] Ernst Wendland, *Exodus*, of The People's Bible series (Milwaukee: Northwestern Publishing House, 1978), p. 92.

Since we are surrounded by such a great cloud of witnesses, let us throw off everything that hinders and the sin that so easily entangles. And let us run with perseverance the race marked out for us, fixing our eyes on Jesus, the pioneer and perfecter of faith. For the joy set before him he endured the cross, scorning its shame, and sat down at the right hand of the throne of God. Consider him who endured such opposition from sinners, so that you will not grow weary and lose heart. (Hebrews 12:1-3)

To stand firm, we go to God's Word to be reminded of God's faithfulness. God worked in the lives of his people all throughout Scripture. Their witness reminds us he will do the same in our lives too.

Instead of becoming trapped in worry and fretting, we fix our eyes on Jesus. Jesus suffered, yes, and so might we, but Jesus' pain served a purpose. There's purpose for our sufferings too. Our sufferings don't pay for our sins as Jesus' suffering did. But in all things God works for the good of those who love him (Romans 8:28). Our sufferings may draw us closer to him, teach us to persevere, work to bring others to faith in Christ, or work in some other way, perhaps in ways we might not realize for years.

For further consideration/discussion:

1. Far too many of us are serial worriers. We waste precious hours unable to sleep and coming up with what-ifs that don't materialize. Where is your focus while worrying?

2. Water is a legitimate need. Very often we have legitimate needs too. What is the last legitimate need you took to God? How did God provide in the moment and in the coming weeks?

3. I have wall hangings and reminders of God's faithfulness all over my house, and yet I can look right past them to focus solely on my circumstances. What tangible things can we do to quit the worry cycle (which often leads to grumbling) and focus on God's faithfulness instead?

God's faithfulness helps us face a new tomorrow

Read Exodus 5:6-14; 16:1-3.

Once the Israelites were free, their recollection of slavery was more pleasant than the actual experience. God delivered them from grueling hours working for slave masters who didn't care about them. A few days in the desert and they were ready to go back.

It's easy to see the Israelites' thanklessness. It's much harder to recognize it in ourselves. Several years ago I was working as a caregiver/companion for an elderly woman. My client was mostly in her right mind, but she was very particular and demanding. She played favorites among the workers. If one worker did something wrong by her standards, she made that person's life miserable until a different worker made her angry.

One day, I was working an early morning shift (4:00–10:30 a.m.). I was exhausted and miserable but unsure how to get out of the situation. She needed round-the-clock care, and there were just a handful of providers. I prayed for the strength to endure and for deliverance.

Through a series of conversations, I was made aware that the Minnesota legislature passed a bill limiting the number of hours and clients a private elderly caregiver/companion could have without being licensed. The licensing process was costly and required ongoing paperwork and supervision by an RN. To continue working the number of hours I was working without a license was against the law. My coworkers decided to keep working in the hopes of not getting caught. Within days of hearing about the bill, I quit working with this client. I kept one person, a friend of my family who was on hospice, as my sole client.

Anytime the temptation to fret about how much less money I was making entered my mind, I told the Lord, "I will not long for the days in the prison now that you have set me free. I will wait on you and trust you to provide." The client in hospice died two months later, and I took on another client part-time. I had better hours, I was paid more per hour, and my new client had a sweet disposition.

It's easy during times of confusion to think it might be better to turn around and go back to what we know, even if what we know wasn't so good. In my situation, to focus on the one good thing, the paycheck, would be to overlook the hours, the way I was treated, my health, and the stress on my family.

The apostle Paul encouraged us to walk "by faith, not by sight" (2 Corinthians 5:7). That means we trust when we don't see or know the outcome. How can we do that? Maybe the place to start is in recognizing that God's love and faithfulness are very different from ours. Psalm 36:5 says, "Your love, Lord, reaches to the heavens, your faithfulness to the skies."

God's love and faithfulness are beyond measure. Our love often has conditions: "As long as you are nice to me, I'll be nice to you." Too often our love is stingy: We do only so much but no more. And our love is selfish: We happily help out if we benefit, but when we don't, we're not so eager. Our faithfulness dwindles, sometimes from sheer laziness. It's too much work to keep up our friendships, to check in on the less fortunate, or to go out of the way to do something for someone else. Not so with God. He doesn't keep a tally of our behavior and cross us off the list when we've reached our bad behavior quota. God never tires of forgiving our sins for Jesus' sake. In Jesus, we always have a second chance.

Jeremiah chronicled the people's stubborn refusal to follow God. Still, God told Jeremiah,

> Stand in the courtyard of the Lord's house and speak to all the people of the towns of Judah who come to worship in the house of the Lord. Tell them everything I command you; do not omit a word. Perhaps they will listen and each

will turn from their evil ways. Then I will relent and not inflict on them the disaster I was planning because of the evil they have done. (Jeremiah 26:2,3)

Jeremiah appealed to the churchgoers: If they listened to God's Word and repented, God would happily relent.

God continues to pursue us with unfathomable faithfulness and love. When we understand that, it changes everything. We sometimes think we've sunk too far for God to want us back. Nothing is further from the truth. When we understand God's faithfulness, we can face whatever changes life brings. God has never left us in the past, and God will not leave us in the future. I love the meme that says, "Be so confident in God's plan that you don't even get upset anymore when things don't go your way." Some of my favorite older Christian women are the ones who have lived long enough to say, "I'm convinced God is even in this!"

For further consideration/discussion:

4. What is going on in our hearts and minds when we long for the past?

5. When the past seems significantly better than the life we have in front of us, we have to make a choice. We can choose to be miserable and make the people around us miserable, or we can choose to see God has a plan even in this (God is faithful). That sounds easier said than done. In reality it's one foot in front of the other—one minute, one hour, and one day at a time. Forget about getting through the month. Look up these promises to get you through today:

• Deuteronomy 31:6 —Often we know we aren't strong enough for what we're facing. How does this passage help?

- Isaiah 49:16 —Too often we feel alone in the midst of struggles. How does this passage help us get through the unknowns of tomorrow?

- 8:38,39 —How does this help us when we're walking through our wilderness stages?

6. Change is monumentally more difficult when we refuse to trust God. The people left Egypt, where they were slaves. They left a country with ample food and went to the desert, where food would be scarcer for a time. God led them to Canaan, a land of abundance. They left abundance and were going to abundance but couldn't see it in the wilderness. Here's why it's so important that we fully understand that God is faithful. If he's not faithful, we can't trust him. If he is, then we can, even when we can't see it. It will dramatically change the way we respond to adversity and change. List the ways you see God's faithfulness in your life right now.

God reveals his faithfulness in his Word

Avid Scripture readers know the Bible is full of rescues. Lot was rescued by Abraham. David defeated Goliath to rescue Israel from Philistine rule. The book of Judges recounts many acts of deliverance. Hezekiah was delivered from the Assyrians. The Jews were spared the destruction Haman plotted. Daniel escaped execution and the lions' den. His friends survived fire. Peter was freed from prison. The apostle Paul escaped death time and again. These instances are just some of the many rescues recorded in Scripture. God knew we would need lots of reassurance. One account could be a fluke.

Very often the person acting as the vehicle of delivery was inadequate, small, weak, or in an impossible situation. Gideon was scared silly. David was considerably smaller than Goliath. Esther really didn't want to be the one to go to the king. God most assuredly wanted us to understand the rescue occurred because of his power and not because of the strength of the rescuer.

God saved his people simply because they were his people. If you've raised children, you know how unlovable they can be at times. There are tantrums and demands and times of obstinance. But you still make sure they have what they need. You feed them and clothe them because they are your children. You love them despite their behavior. And that is exactly how God feels about us.

It's important to note there were times when God didn't deliver his people. Eighty-five priests were killed at the hands of King Saul (1 Samuel 22). Joash killed the faithful priest Zechariah (2 Chronicles 24:22). Job lost his flocks and herds, all of his children, and finally his health (Job 1,2). Stephen was stoned to death (Acts 7:59), and John the Baptist (Matthew 14) and the apostle Paul eventually were beheaded. Even in all these horrific tragedies, God was still faithful. He was faithful to bring those martyred to their heavenly home and faithful to stand by those left behind.

We can be sure we will experience tragedy too. Sometimes the worst happens: we lose the house, a child dies, the crops fail completely. How can we be sure God is faithful even then? Again, we go back to the Word. When God allowed his people to go to captivity in Babylon, he didn't send them alone. He had Daniel and his friends taken to Babylon first. They were trained and given high government positions before the vast majority of Israelites were transported. It would be hard to go to a new land, but God put people in high places who could advocate for the exiles.

Joseph was taken as a slave to Egypt. God had a specific assignment for him—preparing Egypt for the famine that would come. Joseph would save not only the Egyptians but also his own family and many other lives. For a time, he had to be a slave, and for a time, he was in jail, but God made sure Joseph understood that even in prison he was not alone: "The LORD was with him; he showed him kindness and granted him favor in the eyes of the prison warden" (Genesis 39:21).

David lived on the run from Saul for several years. Though Saul pursued him, God never allowed Saul to overtake David. It was not ideal and certainly wouldn't have been David's first choice, but God sustained David. This account and all the others remind us that God works for our good and he promises us he won't leave us. He'll walk with us through the hard times, strengthening and sustaining us.

Maybe the best example of God's faithfulness is found in Psalm 139. David notes that all his ways and all his thoughts are known to God. We are fully known by God and loved completely. No one else knows our every depraved thought, every muttered complaint, and every coarse word we've said. God does and still loves us. Psalm 139:16 says, "All the days ordained for me were written in your book before one of them came to be." We can live with confidence because God knew our ends before we ever took a breath. He could engrave our tombstones before we uttered our first cries. Nothing that happens to us is a shock or surprise to him. God is faithful to carry us through anything life brings and to take us home to heaven.

Every stage is an opportunity to bring glory to God in our words, actions, and attitudes. When we look back, remembering people and days now gone, we can thank the Lord for those he put in our lives and the differences they made for a time. When our tough days come, as they will, we reach out to our Christian friends to be reminded of God's promises and encouraged through the Word.

For further consideration/discussion:

7. Read Psalm 77:1-12. What did Asaph choose to meditate on when he wasn't seeing deliverance?

8. Read 1 Samuel 7:7-12. When the battle was over, Samuel thought it was important to make a visible reminder of God's deliverance for the people to look at. What visible reminders do we have to do the same?

9. The apostle Paul could sing praises in the jail cell at night because God had delivered him often. He had already been driven out of Pisidian Antioch and Iconium and was stoned and left for dead at Lystra. He allowed the hardships of the past to strengthen his resolve to trust in God when the next hardship arose. Some of us don't tell anyone else about the struggles we've faced. Why is that not the best approach? What will it take to open up?

Key takeaways:

+ Instead of grumbling when we suddenly find ourselves in desperate circumstances, we can present our requests to God and wait for his deliverance, knowing he is able to meet each need.

+ Resist the temptation to long for the past. The past had plenty of struggles too, even if we don't remember them. Instead, we ask God for the courage to face whatever is before us and trust he will give us blessings in this phase also.

+ In the Bible we're reminded of God's power and faithfulness in the lives of his people. We can be encouraged he will be with us too!

+ When friends are walking through difficult times, we can remind them of God's power and faithfulness and encourage them to trust and walk by faith.

✝ Find ways to record God's goodness and the way he's provided for you or rescued you from seemingly impossible situations. These can remind you to trust when you face the next impossible situation.

✝ Lots of accounts in the Bible remind us that God works through the weak and feeble. He will use anyone, which means he can use us too!

✝ God works in our lives simply because we are his children and he loves us. We don't have to have our lives under control before he shows up.

✝ God knows everything about us and loves us anyway!

Prayer to close:

Faithful Father, everything we know about faithfulness comes from you. You continue to pull us in as we wander. You love us even when we constantly doubt your love. We complain and you forgive us over and over. Teach us to be more like you, and let us never forget that you are our hope and help. In Jesus' name we pray. Amen.

CHAPTER 4
The Trouble With Stirring Up Trouble

When our discontent creates trouble

Read Numbers 12:1-15.

It happens easily enough. Sometimes I don't even realize I'm doing it. It starts as a bristling in my being. If discontent (Why did he or she do or get or say that?) is not recognized and repented of, it festers into complaints that become bigger the more I discuss them with others. Even after mastering godliness in other areas of my life, this slippery slope is one that's easy enough to slide into.

Up until this point in the exodus from Egypt, we've heard nothing but good things about Miriam. She was the responsible older sister charged with watching Moses in the basket when her mother couldn't keep him any longer (Exodus 2:4). When her brother led the people through the Red Sea, Miriam led the women in praise (Exodus 15:20,21). So what happened?

In a word: discontent. It happens when when we suddenly start noticing our husband's (or child's or employer's) perceived faults. Five, ten, fifteen years of him being a stable, loving spouse (child, employer) disappear when we concentrate on the irritants. *Why can't he be more organized? Does he have to snort as he laughs? Why does he tap his pencil on the table that way?* Idiosyncrasies that once charmed or went unnoticed suddenly annoy and do so even more as we concentrate on them.

What started as complaining and talking behind Moses' back escalated to rebellion. It's the natural progression of uncontrolled discontent. And all too often discontent with one thing leads to discontent with other things. Satan and his army hope that discontent spurs rebellion and causes discord. The apostle Paul offered a different approach. He suggested we "take captive every thought to make it obedient to Christ" (2 Corinthians 10:5).

So often when we're disgruntled, we don't stop to examine what's going on. Recognizing the discontent is an important first step. When we complain, the mouth only reacts to what is in the heart. Jesus said, "A good man brings good things out of the good stored up in his heart, and an evil man brings evil things out of the evil stored up in his heart. For the mouth speaks what the heart is full of" (Luke 6:45).

Do you have a coworker who doesn't feel obligated to do much, which means more work for you? Do your children grumble through the chores you give them? Does your husband ignore everything but what is on TV? The effects of sin often cause discontent and for good reason! A self-absorbed coworker is not working "with all [his] heart, as working for the Lord" (Colossians 3:23). Children who complain and whine over chores aren't modeling God's design: "Children, obey your parents in the Lord, for this is right" (Ephesians 6:1). A negligent husband is a far cry from the apostle Paul's admonition to "love your wives, just as Christ loved the church and gave himself up for her" (Ephesians 5:25).

We can complain constantly over the shortcomings of others, or we can recognize the real problem: "Our struggle is not against flesh and blood, but against the rulers, against the authorities, against the powers of this dark world and against the spiritual forces of evil in the heavenly realms" (Ephesians 6:12). Satan loves discord and broken relationships. He's all too happy to keep us focused on what isn't working.

We'll never be able to rid the world of sin. Complaining rarely brings about the change we seek. "Put on the full armor of God, so that when the day of evil comes, you may be able to stand your ground, and after you have done everything, to stand" (Ephesians 6:13). How can we stand firm without falling into complaining when the world around us is a far cry from what it should be?

The armor the apostle Paul suggests we don consists of remembering your identity as a forgiven child of God with the helmet of salvation. That identity is rooted in God forgiving all your shortcomings. And isn't it true that while we're obsessing over the shortcomings of someone else, we're ignoring our own shortcomings? Salvation isn't dependent on how well we keep God's Word or how worthy we are. Even on our worst days, when we fail miserably, we are loved and forgiven children of God. The person irritating us is also someone loved by God.

The belt of truth will help us see not only our desires in each situation but also the vulnerability of those around us. What are your coworkers going through? Are your children exhausted after a day at school? Is your husband tired from work, worried about finances, or overwhelmed with responsibilities caring for his parents? What sort of role models have they had?

Feet fitted with the gospel will be quick to offer hope in the Lord to all the people around us, even if they aren't doing what we want the way we want. The shield of faith will keep us from falling into Satan's traps when he is spurring us to discontent and reminding us of the inadequacies of those around us. Instead of allowing the issue to become a point of division, we pray instead for unity, peace, and opportunities to bring others into a closer relationship with Christ.

Complaining is ineffective. Not only does it drive a wedge between us and the other person, but it also keeps us from praying, which is far more effective. Eliciting help from God is the very thing that can change hearts, minds, and actions.

I wonder if things might have been different had Miriam gone to Moses and talked about what was bothering her. So often we don't even know we are doing something that drives someone crazy. Instead of letting the annoyance fester to a point of hatred and rebellion, why not see if change is possible?

Or consider coming alongside those God put in your life. If your boss' lack of organization annoys you, ask if you can organize the office or set up a calendar to keep track of everyone's schedules. If your husband struggles to do the projects around the house, maybe doing the projects together would work.

Jesus was patient with impetuous and outspoken Peter. In spite of Peter's shortcomings, Jesus called him and equipped him to become a leader in the early Christian church. Jesus loved and served Judas to the end, even though he knew Judas would betray him. In our sinfulness we can't love to the same degree Jesus did. But God can give us the grace to love and serve those in our lives to a far greater capacity than we're able to do on our own. That will lead to more peaceful relationships and, hopefully, more opportunities to share Jesus with others.

For further consideration/discussion:

1. In what area of your life are you struggling with discontent?

2. Is this discontent an area that requires growth on your part, or is it an inability to be content with what you have? (Being discontent with a weak prayer life is a good thing, but desiring a job that brings prestige while taking you away from your family may be a matter of not being content with God's provision.)

3. We all have people we are patient with and others we aren't. Whom are you impatient with and why?

Make a point to pray for these people to know and love God more. Pray also that you would be patient with them, to facilitate their closer walk with God.

Creating and stirring discontent in others

Read Acts 17:13.

The Jews in this passage tried to stir others against Paul. It's easy to think that's something we never do. We may not even know we do it. It happens when we say things like "Wow! I would never let my child do that!" or "How do you put up with a boss who does that?"

I've learned that our lives are all different and what works for one family wouldn't work for the next. What one company sees as standard is very different from another. We all have different thresholds for dealing with sins and weaknesses. Maybe your husband or best friend overspends or is embarrassingly loud and boisterous or overanalyzes everything. Maybe this person over-eats or abuses alcohol or complains incessantly or easily falls into despair. What you see as an asset (he loves my home cooking!) another would see as a liability (I don't want to cook!) and vice versa. What would make one woman climb the walls another can handle. Oh, we all wish we had a perfect spouse, landlord, children, and boss! Our spouses, landlords, children, and bosses surely wish the same was true of us.

At the point of finding fault with someone, it's good to stop and consider our own shortcomings and faults. My husband's generosity has miffed me on more than one occasion. Rarely does he refuse when his kids ask for something. He's likely to buy lunch or coffee for a coworker. He often refuses to take money after spending hours fixing something for someone. I have chided him for giving in to the kids instead of recognizing him as the loving father wanting to provide well and even lavish his children with gifts. O God, help me to hold my tongue! Remind me through my husband that you too love to lavish gifts on your children.

A gentle and quiet spirit will not only keep us from stirring trouble up for others but will also stop others when they try to stir us up. When someone calls to report another's bad behavior, we could add to the information, reporting something equally scandalous about the person or someone else. Or we could remind the caller that grace is the greatest gift and that we too fall short daily.

Sometimes we jump to conclusions or assume something that stirs up nonexistent trouble. When we don't have all the facts, it's important to recognize that things may not be what they seem. Instead of leaping to the worst-case scenario, it's better to heed Luther's instruction in the explanation to the Eighth Commandment: "We should fear and love God that we do not tell lies about our neighbor, betray him, or give him a bad name, but defend him, speak well of him, and take his words and actions in the kindest possible way." [3]

As we're chatting with friends, we have the opportunity to lovingly encourage them to stay the course and see the good in their spouse and children and situation rather than just the bad. We can sympathize with their frustration while reminding them of the importance of grace. It's important to remember that this spouse and these children and even the struggles at work are because we have been blessed with a spouse, children, and a job. When we're able to overlook faults and treat people with grace and love, we keep the door open to tell them about far more important and eternal matters. Jesus' unconditional love and forgiveness enabled him to accept tax collectors and prostitutes (something the Pharisees could not do). He saw them as souls in need of a Savior, which eventually led some of them to leave their lives of sin. May God give us the strength to do the same.

For further consideration/discussion:

4. In what seemingly innocent ways can we stir up trouble for our friends' faith walks?

5. The Jews in Thessalonica had a mission to stir up trouble for Paul, and they were willing to travel to do so. We don't have to travel anymore to stir up trouble. How can we stir up trouble right from the comfort of our homes?

---

[3] *Luther's Catechism*, p. 97.

6. Why might it be easier to stir up trouble on the phone or computer than it is to do it in person?

7. What steps can we take to support our friends and build them up to appreciate their situations rather than spurring them on to discontent?

Satan as the ultimate troublemaker

Read Genesis 3:1-4.

If you want to defeat your enemy, it's good to know how your enemy works. Satan is crafty. He tempted Eve to question God's Word and insinuated that God was keeping her from a better life even while she lived in the perfection of the Garden of Eden. He uses the same technique on us. "Did God really say till death do you part? Did he really say submit to those in authority? He couldn't have meant your husband or your boss."

Satan is also opportunistic. The apostle Peter describes him as a lion looking for someone to devour (1 Peter 5:8). He and his army prey on us when we're tired and weak and overwhelmed. He reminds us of past hurts and attempts to separate us from Christians who would help us.

Jesus referred to Satan as a liar and the father of lies. Remember that the next time you're fixating on another's faults and allowing your discontentment to fester. Thoughts like, *If he loved me, he wouldn't do that* or *My boss doesn't appreciate all my hard work* or *Why is my child the only one who does this?* are usually not accurate. They tempt us to despair instead of seeing the good our husband, boss, or child does.

And if Satan can't get us to be discontent with everyone else in our lives, he'll remind us of all the times we've stirred up trouble in the past to drive us to despair. For that we must look to the cross. The reformer Martin Luther is quoted as saying, "So when the devil throws your sins in your face and declares that you deserve death and hell, tell him this: 'I admit that I deserve death and hell, what of it? For I know One who suffered and made satisfaction on my behalf. His name is Jesus Christ, Son of God, and where He is there I shall be also!'"[4]

When I remember that Satan is the real enemy and my spouse, my friend, my child, or my boss is not, I'm more likely to pray for those in my life, overlook their shortcomings, and keep things in the proper perspective. A bad day is not the end of the relationship. It's just a bad day.

Jesus used the same approach when Peter suggested that Jesus didn't have to die. Jesus didn't make Peter his enemy. He proclaimed, "Get behind me, Satan!" (Matthew 16:23). Jesus was telling Peter that Satan was behind his words. Rather than allowing these words to destroy their relationship, Jesus forgave Peter and continued to treat him as his disciple. Jesus washed Peter's feet in the upper room. Then he instituted the Lord's Supper as evidence of his love and commitment to take away Peter's sin. When that relentless love and continual forgiveness are reflected in our relationships, we will profit as much or more than the other person. Genuine and sincere relationships withstand squabbles, disagreements, and disappointments when we encourage and build up the other person.

For further consideration/discussion:

8. One way to get out of the slump of discontent is to look for the good in others and be thankful for them. When you're angry at your child, consider the things you love about that child. When you are annoyed at your spouse, thank God for the things your spouse has added to your life. Doing so pushes Satan out of your thoughts so you can focus on the way the Lord has blessed you through them. What good can you find right now in someone you've struggled to love?

---

[4] Martin Luther, *Luther: Letters of Spiritual Counsel*, translated and edited by Theodore G. Tappert (London: SCM Press and Philadelphia: The Westminster Press, 1955; reprint, Vancouver: Regent College Publishing, 2003), p. 85.

9. Jesus could read the thoughts of those around him. Since we don't have Jesus in person correcting our misinformed thoughts, what can we do to make sure we aren't making false assumptions or jumping to a conclusion that isn't true?

10. James 4:7 says, "Resist the devil, and he will flee from you." Satan is a powerful enemy, but we've been given the weapons we need to fight him. Consider the full armor of God in Ephesian 6:14-18. How is this going to help you when discontent bubbles up and spurs you to rebellion?

Key takeaways:

+ When we have a problem with people, it's best to talk to them and discuss a peaceful resolution or choose to overlook an incident instead of making it into a major ordeal.

+ Pray daily for contentment.

+ Prodding others to discontent is a sin.

+ Satan loves to stir up trouble and fuel the fire. If we recognize his traps, we're less likely to fall into them.

+ We have been given the power to resist Satan.

Prayer to close:

Dear Father in heaven, forgive me for too often being discontent and finding fault with those in my life. Help me to see the good instead of dwelling on the bad. When the army of evil stirs my heart to discontent, let me recognize it and resist it. Help me to help others in this endeavor and to be a voice of grace in a judgmental world. In Jesus' powerful name I pray. Amen.

CHAPTER 5

How to Deal With Sensitive Information

The toll of gossip

Read Esther 3:1-9.

Gossip is defined as "idle talk or rumor, especially about the personal or private affairs of others."[5] Gossip doesn't have to be about a person's sin. It may be about a shortcoming or weakness. Or it may reveal details the person would rather people didn't know. It is exposing what was meant to be private or telling on someone for the purpose of stirring up trouble.

A rumor is different than gossip. A rumor is information that circulates but isn't necessarily true. We tend to think of rumors and gossip as fairly harmless. In truth, both rumors and gossip can be equally damaging.

In the account in Esther, gossip and rumors converged. The situation started when Mordecai refused to bow to Haman and, in so doing, disobeyed the command of the king. Werner Franzmann explains in his *Bible History Commentary: Old Testament*, "The Persian kings...demanded divine honor for themselves. They also demanded such honor be accorded their highest officials.... Mordecai refused to give Haman the homage that belongs only to God."[6]

---

[5] www.dictionary.com, s.v. "gossip."

[6] Werner Franzmann, *Bible History Commentary: Old Testament* (Milwaukee: Northwestern Publishing House, 1980), p. 555.

Mordecai refused to bow in the same way Shadrach, Meshach, and Abednego refused to bow to the statue of gold that King Nebuchadnezzar erected. The event, detailed in Daniel chapter 3, tells us Nebuchadnezzar set up the image and demanded that all the leaders of his kingdom worship it. As leader of the vast Babylonian Empire, Nebuchadnezzar was proclaiming his god Bel to be the ultimate god. Shadrach, Meshach, and Abednego couldn't obey such a command. Their refusal attracted the attention of men who told on them. What was the intent behind telling on Shadrach, Meshach, and Abednego? Franzmann explains, "We need not search far for the reason why some of the magicians and sorcerers brought charges against the three friends of Daniel. Though they owed their lives to them and Daniel, they were extremely jealous of the three, because these young men had been promoted to high positions ahead of themselves, who were much older men."[7]

In Mordecai's case we aren't given any indication the royal officials were jealous of Mordecai. Their motive seems to be altogether different. These men spoke to Mordecai concerning the matter "day after day." When he refused to conform, they finally told Haman "to see whether Mordecai's behavior would be tolerated, for he had told them he was a Jew" (Esther 3:4). In Esther chapter 1, Vashti refused to come before the king when summoned and was banished for disobedience. Would Mordecai's disobedience be tolerated, or would he be made an example as well?

The royal officials were miffed at Mordecai's behavior. But when Haman found out, he was incensed. Motivated by violent, uncontrollable anger and "vengeful lust,"[8] Haman manipulated the facts and offered rumors about the Jews to King Xerxes to convince the king to annihilate the Jews.

As with most rumors, part of what Haman told Xerxes was true. The Jews' customs were different from the other people of the kingdom, and in this one instance, Mordecai didn't obey the command of the king. But that is where the truth of the rumor ended. Haman indicated that the Jews set out to deliberately disobey the laws. He made it appear as if he had Persia's best interest at heart. In

---

[7] Franzmann, p. 539.
[8] Franzmann, p. 555.

truth, pride and a desire for retribution fueled his plan to dispose of Mordecai and the entire Jewish race. Hatred fueled his lies. Haman may have fooled Xerxes, but God knew! Proverbs 16:2 says, "All a person's ways seem pure to them, but motives are weighed by the LORD."

Just as God saw Haman's heart, he sees our hearts too. What motivates us to gossip and spread rumors? Concern may lead us to pray for someone and even seek counsel for the best way to help; but gossip, whether deliberate or not, damages another's character. In the Eighth Commandment, Martin Luther encourages us to defend our neighbors, speak well of them, and take their words and actions in the kindest possible way.

It's easy enough to exaggerate people's words or actions to make them look worse than they may be. Our sinful nature often sees and assumes the worst in others. It happens in political and social gossip. And it happens when we make sweeping generalizations about "those people" without evidence or even reliable sources. One video or headline is all it takes to plant seeds of disparaging information that lead us to judge and condemn.

What can we do when we hear gossip about politicians, athletes, or entertainers, especially since it isn't always possible to fact-check? We can't call them to get their side of the story or to see if there's any truth to what is being said. We can't talk to eyewitnesses to determine what happened. While we might not be able to get to the bottom of the gossip, we can refuse to share it. When we read unseemly news about people of status, we can start by praying for them. The apostle Paul urges us that "petitions, prayers, intercession and thanksgiving be made for all people—for kings and all those in authority, that we may live peaceful and quiet lives in all godliness and holiness" (1 Timothy 2:1,2).

It shouldn't surprise us when those of money and influence aren't living with Christian values. But it's also important to recognize we only have a portion of the story and even that portion comes at the expense of someone's reputation and dignity.

The Pharisees and teachers of the law brought a woman to Jesus who had been caught in the act of adultery. They did not bring the man, and the *Concordia Self-Study Bible* notes the matter could have been taken care of privately. The leaders paraded the woman through the crowded temple courts in a deliberate act to humiliate her.[9] In response to this, Jesus reminded all those gathered that they also were sinners: "Let any of you who is without sin be the first to throw a stone at her" (John 8:7).

I, for one, am thankful my sins aren't on display. As we remember this, empathy motivates us to pray for all involved and determine not to be part of spreading the gossip further.

For further consideration/discussion:

1. It's easy to see that jealousy motivated the wise men to tell Nebuchadnezzar about Daniel's friends and that pride and hatred motivated Haman. What are the motivations for printing gossip and rumors about the leaders of our country and those in the entertainment industry?

2. There are times when it is necessary to get to the bottom of a rumor about a leader, just as Mordecai uncovered the plot against the king (Esther 2:21) and Esther told the king the truth about Haman (Esther 7). What things should we keep in mind as the truth is being uncovered?

3. Is there ever a time when it's a good idea to get involved in the gossip and rumors of the entertainment industry or political world, even when you don't know the particulars?

---

[9] Robert G. Hoerber, editor, *Concordia Self-Study Bible* (St. Louis: Concordia Publishing House, 1986), p. 1,621.

When you know something about someone else

Read Proverbs 11:13; 26:20.

Every time we hear or witness damaging, demeaning, or personal news concerning someone, we have to choose what to do with that information. Years ago, I was telling a few other women at church about a tragedy another person had been through. I was in the middle of the story when the person the story was about entered the room, clearly not impressed with my details and added observations. It was an important lesson I needed to learn. When the temptation to gossip arises, just imagine that person in the room with you. How would that change the way you talk about that person? Would you bring up the person or the situation at all?

There are times when it is imperative to share information, particularly if someone is in danger or a crime has been committed. When a former church leader was arrested for buying child pornography, transparency was important. Creating an open dialogue in the church gave us the opportunity to work through the sorrow of a friend falling for Satan's schemes. Our youth needed the leaders of the church to come alongside them. To hide the information or refuse to talk about it would have invalidated their feelings and left them unequipped to deal with their questions. We wouldn't have been able to pray with our young people and talk about the trust that had rightfully been shaken.

As children mature, it can be hard to know what needs to be shared with the family and what doesn't. When one child makes a bad choice or breaks a rule, it isn't necessarily important for the whole house to know what happened. Children have to feel safe to come to us when they make poor choices so we can work through better options. We want them to trust us with their failings.

Other times the siblings need to know what transpired, especially if the consequences will affect them. That doesn't mean all the details have to be made public. Discretion will save the offending child from humiliation while giving the other children needed information. As the third child in my family, I often learned what not to do by watching the choices my older siblings made and seeing the consequences of those choices. It's only been in adulthood that I've come to learn details I wasn't given at the time.

There are times at work and in churches and other organizations when it is important people don't know everything going on behind the scenes. It can be hard in those instances for everyone involved. It's hard for those who don't have all the information and are trying to understand what's happening based on the bits they know. It can also be hard for the people who have all the information and are working behind the scenes.

When people say things without full knowledge of the situation, it puts those who know in a difficult spot. Do you betray the confidence of the situation in order to justify your actions, or do you listen and empathize while keeping private matters confidential?

Jesus had access to everyone's thoughts and motives. Yet in the gospels we have only a few instances of Jesus exposing them. When he did, it was for the sake of others or because he saw that others had in mind to do something that wasn't according to the Father's will.

After Jesus fed five thousand people by multiplying the loaves and fishes, John told us that "Jesus, knowing that they intended to come and make him king by force, withdrew again to a mountain by himself" (John 6:15). Jesus didn't come to be an earthly king, much to the disappointment of many. He also didn't come to be the earthly provider for the Jews so they would never be physically hungry again. His mission was to be our Redeemer, paying for our sins so we could be in heaven for eternity. To avoid any confusion about his purpose or his Father's will, Jesus quietly left and went his own way. He didn't announce his good intentions. He didn't expose the folly of those who didn't understand. He simply left that region and continued his ministry elsewhere. Mark tells us of another situation where Jesus reacted to people's thoughts:

> When Jesus saw their faith, he said to the paralyzed man, "Son, your sins are forgiven."
> Now some teachers of the law were sitting there, thinking to themselves, "Why does this fellow talk like that? He's blaspheming! Who can forgive sins but God alone?"

Immediately Jesus knew in his spirit that this was what they were thinking in their hearts, and he said to them, "Why are you thinking these things? Which is easier: to say to this paralyzed man, 'Your sins are forgiven,' or to say, 'Get up, take your mat and walk'? But I want you to know that the Son of Man has authority on earth to forgive sins." So he said to the man, "I tell you, get up, take your mat and go home." (Mark 2:5-11)

The People's Bible explains, "Jesus read the man's heart and knew something infinitely worse than paralysis was troubling him—his sins. . . . That's why the Lord first met that need, even as forgiveness is the greatest need of our hearts." Pastor Wicke explained further, "In a contemptuous way [the teachers of the law] speak of [Jesus] as 'this fellow.' They were indeed correct when they said, 'Who can forgive sins but God alone?' But they were wrong when they said, 'He's blaspheming!'"[10]

Jesus didn't heal the man to show the teachers his power. He was showing them and all those present that he was the Son of God, sent from the Father to do a miracle far greater than healing a man's broken body. He would pay for our sins and give us access to God's presence, something we were completely powerless to do, much like the paralytic was powerless to stand up and walk on his own.

Jesus could have continually exposed the sinful thoughts of those around him. But he didn't. Christian love leads us to leave gossip unspoken as well. If our words come at the expense of another's reputation, or if we have to announce the other's shortcomings or weakness to make us look better, we are motivated by our sinful nature rather than Christ's love. When we understand how amazing God's grace for us is, then we will understand why God's grace rests on others as well. Grace spurs us to walk alongside others, lifting them as they struggle.

Sometimes information comes to us whether we are looking for it or not. My mother is quick to point out that as hard as some information is to hear, once we know it, we know how to pray.

---

[10] Harold E. Wicke, *Mark*, of The People's Bible series (Milwaukee: Northwestern Publishing House, 1984), pp. 34,35.

When we hear something about someone that we wish we hadn't, instead of falling into despair, we can fall into battle formation, taking our requests to God in prayer.

For further consideration/discussion:

4. What is the difference between going to someone with gossip and going to a trusted friend with a legitimate concern or complaint about another person?

5. Is there a time to tell a trusted friend the backstory of a situation, or is breaking the confidence of another an absolute no-no?

6. My natural tendency is to shut down when I hear disparaging information about someone I love. When a relative brazenly admitted embracing sin at a family function, my mom simply responded by saying, "Now we know how to pray." How do we fortify ourselves to deal with information we wish wasn't true?

When gossip and rumors hit home

Read 1 Samuel 20:1-4.

Perhaps one of the most crucial lessons we learn is figuring out who to trust with our secrets. We all need someone we can lean on, someone we can tell our hurts and our frustrations to. When you find that person, you will never think lightly of it again.

David went to Jonathan with the news that Jonathan's father, King Saul, was trying to kill David. Jonathan wouldn't believe Saul would want to kill his best friend. In response, David and Jonathan hatched a plan to find the truth.

Our good friends will do the same. When they hear something negative or embarrassing or damaging about us, they will find us to talk about it, as David did. Whether the gossip is true or not, our dear friends will advise us what to do next and how to do it. They will surround us with prayer and encouragement.

Not everyone will have our best intentions in mind, but hopefully we will find a Christian community that does. At one time or another, we all will experience embarrassing situations we never wanted to be in. Sometimes our actions brought it on. Other times, we did nothing to cause what happened. When the Christian community meets you with empathy and support, even our worst moments are so much more bearable.

Others may meet us with condescending glares and whispers. Sometimes the gossip reaches those we love. What do we do then? Humility is a good place to start. No one is above the consequences of bad choices. Better to admit it, deal with it, and move on than try to excuse or cover up the situation.

And what do we do when we didn't do anything to cause the tragedy? When Job experienced terrible tragedy—first in the loss of his livelihood, then in the death of his ten children, and finally in the decline of his health—Job's friends accused him of sin. In his friends' eyes, Job's circumstances were the consequence of wrongdoing known only to God. They were wrong in their assumption. James 5:11 commends Job for his patient perseverance through all of this.

In Numbers chapter 12, Miriam and Aaron spoke against Moses. They undermined his leadership by criticizing his choice of a Cushite wife. Moses was so humble that he did not respond, so God intervened on his behalf. Sometimes our best response to verbal attacks is to humbly wait for God to intervene.

Who knows God's plan for our lives? When the gossip against us is strong, we may be rescued immediately or after a season or maybe never. We may have to leave the situation—or in drastic cases, leave town. Maybe we can't get together with family for a time. Even though we have prayed and tried, if things go from bad to worse, then we rely on God to work out what we can't.

Relentless persecution can lead to seasons of great spiritual growth if we submerse ourselves in God's Word, prayer, and a posture of humility. At the end of the ugly seasons, we will be equipped to be the friend who "sticks closer than a brother" (Proverbs 18:24) when others find themselves in a similar situation. We'll know how to encourage and give godly counsel and to stay with and comfort the broken as they navigate difficult situations.

For further consideration/discussion:

7. The apostle Peter gives us this advice: "Live such good lives among the pagans that, though they accuse you of doing wrong, they may see your good deeds and glorify God on the day he visits us" (1 Peter 2:12). Taking Peter's words to heart may not keep us from being victims of gossip and rumors. In fact, it may be the reason the unbelieving world turns on us. How so?

8. What is the greatest thing you can tell a friend who has fallen into a sin and becomes the center of gossip?

9. What do you do when you find out a friend is saying untrue things about you, things that could damage your reputation?

Key takeaways:

✝ Gossip is intimate information that is shared with others at the expense of the person it is about. Rumors may contain bits of truth along with lies.

✝ When we hear gossip and rumors about politicians and those in the entertainment industry, it's important to realize that we don't have the whole picture. It's also important to remember that those who reported the information were likely paid to reveal it.

✝ If it's important information that is pertinent to our country, we need to give investigators time to figure out the truth. In the meantime, we can do our part by refusing to pass rumors and gossip along while praying for God to bring the truth to light.

✝ Martin Luther encourages us to defend our friends and neighbors. We can encourage them instead of tearing them down and telling others damaging information about them.

✝ We can always pray. God knows the particulars of every situation.

✝ Going to a trusted friend to seek counsel concerning another person, even if it's an intimate matter, isn't gossip. If possible, keep the person's identity anonymous. Godly friends can help us see a situation clearly and give us advice as to how to proceed.

Prayer to close:

Once again, heavenly Father, we see how our mouths can do great damage or bring about great healing. Help us find the right person to talk to if something needs to be shared. And help us discern when to be silent and let you take care of the situation. Forgive us for so often spreading information for the sake of conversation. Help us learn to do better with the Spirit's help and through the power of Christ. Amen.

CHAPTER 6
Speaking the Truth in Love

Hypocrisy distorts truth

Read Mark 12:13-17.

Jesus told his disciples he was the Way, the Truth, and the Life (John 14:6). Thomas Chisholm, who penned the song "Great Is Thy Faithfulness," put it this way: "There is no shadow of turning with you." We don't have to worry about God changing his mind or switching directions or realizing he was wrong when the truth comes out. He doesn't change his mind because he knows the truth, and he proclaims the truth because he is truth.

Satan loves division, and he loves to use our words as weapons to fuel polarization. In the exchange we read about in Mark, Jesus saw through the religious leaders' cunning and used truth to cut through rhetoric and schemes. If the Pharisees believed he was a man of integrity who taught "the way of God in accordance with the truth" (Mark 12:14), why would they be trying to catch him in order to bring him down?

Hypocrisy is a disparity between actions and words. It is the word secular circles most often use to describe churchgoers. For that reason and because it is a trait of Satan (not God), we would do well to understand it better.

When Jesus spoke, you could be sure what he said was truth. On various occasions the Jewish leaders tried to force Jesus to pick an earthly side. In their limited perspective, you had to choose between Rome or the Jews. If Jesus taught and acted purely in support of the Jews, that may give the leaders leverage against him with Rome. To support Rome was professional suicide among the Jews, who hated being governed by Rome. Asking Jesus for the truth in this circumstance when they were not interested in the truth demonstrated their hypocrisy.

On a different occasion, the teachers of the law and the Pharisees brought a woman caught in adultery to Jesus in an effort to force him to choose between Moses' teaching and Roman rule. Their case? "In the Law Moses commanded us to stone such women. Now what do you say?" (John 8:5). In their limited perspective, Jesus had two choices, and either choice would be political suicide. If Jesus told them to follow the Law of Moses, they could accuse him of not caring about Roman law. If he said to let her go, they would accuse him of not caring about the Law of Moses. The *Concordia Self-Study Bible* points out that this particular law only called for death in the case of a virgin engaged to be married, and both parties, not just the woman, were to be put to death.[11]

Hypocrisy can look pious. It can give the appearance of acting on behalf of justice. Jesus saw what they were doing at the expense of that woman. The Jewish leaders humiliated the woman publicly in the temple courts where crowds had gathered to listen to Jesus. True justice in this situation would involve the man who committed adultery being held responsible as well. And if the Pharisees were concerned with the spiritual health of either party, they would have dealt with the situation privately, behind closed doors, out of the watchful eyes of the crowds.

Jesus didn't deny there had been sin. He didn't disregard the Law of Moses or Roman authority. Instead, he called out sin not only in the woman but also in all of us who are eager to point out another's sin while neglecting our own careless actions.

It's easy for us to fall into this trap of judging others. Jesus said in Matthew 7:1,2, "Do not judge, or you too will be judged. For in the same way you judge others, you will be judged, and with the measure you use, it will be measured to you." It's easy to point to

[11] Hoerber, p. 1,621.

the sins of others as a sign of moral decay while being oblivious to our own sin. *They* need to change. *They* are a threat to society. *They* should learn to be more like us. We are quick to turn up our noses at *their* sins while flagrantly turning a blind eye to *our* sins.

Thank God his grace extends to all sinners! And thank God he works to open our eyes to our faults. To live in truth is to recognize that we have fallen short and need God's grace just as much as the next person. As we do this, we'll be far less prone to drag others in front of the crowd to call out their sin. We'll focus on dealing with our own sin and be quick to extend grace, rather than judgment, to fellow sinners and redeemed saints.

Integrity will spur us to go one step further. We act with integrity when we mean what we say and do what we say we will, even if it comes at a price and even if it means we suffer loss because of it. Joseph ran away from Potiphar's wife. He meant what he said when he declared he had no intention of sleeping with her. He ran away even if it meant losing his job and ending up in prison. Daniel didn't stop praying to God even when it became illegal to do so. It could have cost him everything.

We can hardly expect the world to live with integrity, but it saddens us when we fail to see it in ourselves. The disciples said they would stand with Jesus, but instead they fled from him in the garden. Each of us will have opportunities to stand up and stand out for God's ways. And we will need the strength that God provides to stand.

For further consideration/discussion:

1. Think of the last argument/disagreement you had with a believer. What truth were you overlooking in the heat of the moment because you were so bent on defending your side?

2. Long ago I determined not to fight with unbelievers. The apostle Paul told Timothy, "Don't have anything to do with foolish and stupid arguments, because you know they produce quarrels. And the Lord's servant must not be quarrelsome but must

be kind to everyone, able to teach, not resentful. Opponents must be gently instructed, in the hope that God will grant them repentance leading them to a knowledge of the truth" (2 Timothy 2:23-25). Circle the key words in that passage. Which ones do you need to work on?

3. If you can be completely transparent, what has kept you from digging deeper into the Word? (It is in the Word that we're going to recognize our sin and be filled with sorrow for the sins of others.)

Speaking the truth in love

Read John 4:1-26,39-42.

The woman at the well was no doubt used to hearing empty promises. Five failed marriages had to have brought disappointment after disappointment after disappointment. She found another man, maybe one who told her what she wanted to hear. Or maybe this one told her the truth: that he had no intention of marrying her, but at least for a time he'd be her companion. And Jesus, instead of saying what she wanted to hear, brought up her greatest disappointment and likely her greatest source of shame. How would she answer this stranger who asked her to get her husband? She could tell him the truth without telling him the whole truth. It was true, after all, that she had no husband.

Like this woman, we can usually get away with not being *completely* honest. We can say that our marriage or our children are fine, even when they are not entirely fine. We can weave stories on social media that tell the world what we want them to think, even if that is a far cry from reality. We can fill our Christmas letters with partial truths to create an impressive narrative. But God knows the truth, the whole and sometimes ugly truth. And while we don't have to divulge our issues to everyone we meet, there is something to be said for an honest response. It's okay, and even refreshing, when "How are you?" is met with a humble but truthful "It's been a rough week."

In fact, it was the truth spoken in love that drew the woman to Jesus. Instead of avoiding her as so many others would, he told her what she already knew. She was broken and desperately in need of a Savior.

It's as easy as that, and yet we so often mess it up. Either we shrug off truth because we don't want to jeopardize our relationship with our friend, coworker, stepdaughter, etc., or we use angry and ugly words, speaking the truth in hate. The apostle Paul says doing that makes all our other efforts worthless:

> If I speak in the tongues of men or of angels, but do not have love, I am only a resounding gong or a clanging cymbal. If I have the gift of prophecy and can fathom all mysteries and all knowledge, and if I have a faith that can move mountains, but do not have love, I am nothing. If I give all I possess to the poor and give over my body to hardship that I may boast, but do not have love, I gain nothing. (1 Corinthians 13:1-3)

If love isn't the motivator, then our words will be a hammer. When we really understand that the Word is the truth and life, it isn't something we use to beat people down and keep them in guilt over their sin. God's truth is a ladder to bring those we love out of the pit of sin.

Deception keeps us in bondage. As long as we believe God doesn't love us and Jesus' death doesn't cover our sin, we won't know our identity in Christ. It is equally tragic to somehow think that we are better than others and that Jesus' death doesn't cover their sin. We want all people to know that they "are a chosen people, a royal priesthood, a holy nation, God's special possession" (1 Peter 2:9).

Once we know and believe it, we'll want others to understand that their sin is covered too. They are no worse sinners than we are.

And they are no less forgiven than we are. Love for our neighbor will cause us to lead our friends and loved ones to Jesus, not to win an argument but because it's the way of freedom from bondage to sin. It's the way of eternal life. Satan wants to keep us deceived, drawing up battle lines and taking shots at the other person. Jesus wants us to find rest in the peace and freedom from sin he offers.

It's hard to find truth in the world. I often struggle to know what to believe. Some news sources say one thing; others say something else. What I watch and read doesn't always line up with what I see. Our culture doesn't care about truth. My truth, the way I see something or what I experience, might be vastly different from your truth. And by secular standards, that's okay. Pastor Mike from Time of Grace reminded me that Jesus didn't say that he was *a* truth or one way to the truth or *his* truth. He said he was *the* truth.

Sometimes our struggle to find truth is because we forget to look where truth can be found. We spend hours scrolling through Facebook, Instagram, and our favorite streaming network but put so little time into knowing and understanding the Word. Tools like The People's Bible commentaries, study Bibles, our pastors, and essays from the seminary exist and are at our disposal. But often we'd rather seek the pleasure of the world than search the depth of the Word of God.

Jesus is the truth that the people of the world are looking for even when they don't know it. We are truth-bearers, and we can show the world a better way.

For further consideration/discussion:

4. We've all had times when our confrontations have been less than loving. What keeps you from speaking the truth in a loving manner?

5. A dear friend and mentor asked me to go to a Christian women's conference with her. After serious Bible teaching and time spent in worship and prayer, we headed to dinner. We were

deep in our discussion when she suggested I needed to change some things in my life. I wasn't offended. In fact, I was grateful for her insight and took her words to heart. What can we learn from this approach?

6. As you read the gospels, you might note that Jesus didn't approach people to let them know the ways they could improve their lives. He didn't tell Peter he'd had enough of his antics or tell James and John they really needed to work on their tempers. Yet Jesus always spoke the truth, and he was an expert at changing hearts. What was his method?

Lying to God

Read Acts 4:36–5:10.

Presumably, Barnabas' act of selling land and giving the money to the disciples brought him a bit of attention in the early church. Ananias and Sapphira wanted that attention. Like Barnabas, they sold land. Like Barnabas, they brought the money to the disciples. The problem was twofold. First, they sought earthly recognition, and second, they were willing to lie to get it. When they brought the money to the disciples, they gave a portion of what they received for the land but claimed to have given it all.

If you're a little unsure what it means to test the Holy Spirit, The People's Bible explains: "The couple had tested the Spirit of the Lord in the way children test a new teacher—to see what they could get away with, to see how far they could stretch the goodness of God. Tragically, Ananias and Sapphira learned that God will not be deceived, and he will not let his grace be abused. Better for us to learn it from this story than by experience."[12]

---

[12] Richard D. Balge, *Acts*, of The People's Bible series (Milwaukee: Northwestern Publishing House, 1984), p. 58.

Peter said Satan had filled Ananias' and Sapphira's hearts. Jesus told his disciples that Satan has "no truth in him. When he lies, he speaks his native language, for he is a liar and the father of lies" (John 8:44).

Years ago, I went to Vietnam for ten days. Except for the tour guide, no one outside of my group spoke English. On the few occasions when I heard English, I was drawn to these people because they spoke my native tongue. When we lie, exaggerate, or manipulate the truth, Satan hears his native language. Carefully consider whose language you want to speak. If you've developed a tendency to say what people want to hear or what you need to say to get your way, you are inadvertently aligning yourself with the devil. His pleasures are temporary and very often a smoke screen that disappears with the consequences of the sin we fall into.

You might be thinking that you never lie to God and so this really doesn't apply to you. I like to think that too. But if I'm completely honest, sometimes I do lie to God. I lie to him in my prayers when I point out the sins of others without confessing my own sin and my own part in the ordeal. *Look at them, Lord! See how evil they are! Are you going to let them get away with that?*

God sees how evil *they* are, and he sees how evil I am. He sees the thoughts and motives of everyone involved. Proverbs 16:2 says, "All a person's ways seem pure to them, but motives are weighed by the LORD." When I pray, God is concerned about my heart. Maybe I do have reason for anger. Maybe injustice has been done. God sees, and God knows. Several times in the psalms, David asked God to search him. If I'm honest, I don't always want God to do that. I don't want to acknowledge that I'm being self-centered or arrogant or that I'm keeping track of others' sins without acknowledging my own.

Scripture tells us Daniel was a righteous man. In Daniel chapter 6, his enemies could find nothing that he was doing wrong. Yet when Daniel prayed for Israel, he didn't pray for the sins of his fellow Jews and how evil they had been. He prayed, "[Lord,] we have sinned and done wrong. We have been wicked and have rebelled; we have turned away from your commands and laws. We have not listened to your servants the prophets" (Daniel 9:5,6). Daniel recognized that "all have sinned and fall short of the glory of God" hundreds of years before the apostle Paul penned those words (Romans 3:23).

We lie to ourselves when we think *they* are the problem without realizing our own sinful tendencies. Humility will lead us to be more like David, asking God to search us. And humility will lead us to be more like Daniel, acknowledging our sins as God shows us. *We* are sinful. *We* have gone astray. *We* add to the chaos we experience because we stray from God's perfect ways.

God's truth is a balm that heals what sin steals. We have no reason to lie to God because he knows the truth. Satan will convince us that we don't need God and have done nothing wrong. God's truth not only shows us our sin, but it also shows us a Savior who went to great lengths to pay for that sin. The truth about us is not always convenient or easy, but it is always the better way. Any truth, as ugly as it may appear, shows our need for God. And God is waiting for us when we come to that understanding.

For further consideration/discussion:

7. Have you ever tried to convince God how horrible someone was? Have you stretched the truth in your prayers to make your case stronger? What is that showing God?

8. We all lie. Maybe we don't deliberately lie, but we exaggerate. The words *always* and *never* often indicate dishonesty. Or perhaps we twist the facts to get what we want. Maybe you've fallen into the habit of making promises but then go back on your word. In what ways do you struggle with honesty?

9. I struggle with being brazenly truthful. One of my core strengths is strategy, so I often see and understand what a problem is before others do. It's taken me a long time to realize not everyone wants to know the truth and there's a time and

a way to tell it. How do we know when to say something and when to refrain from saying anything?

Key takeaways:

† Hypocrisy is a form of lying. It's saying one thing but meaning or acting differently.

† Jesus showed us that speaking the truth doesn't necessarily mean taking sides. Often there is some truth on both sides.

† Jesus was an expert in showing love. He often spent time with people. He went to the homes of sinners and stayed at the well to meet the woman. He spent time with sinners in order to love them while speaking the truth.

† We can't lie to God, so we might as well be honest with our prayers. David, Habakkuk, and other Scripture writers show us that it's fine to go to God with our honest complaints, sorrows, and disappointments while also, like Daniel, recognizing our own faults and weaknesses.

† Satan does his best to keep us from the truth because he knows the truth will give us comfort and hope. Recognizing him as the father of lies is a good deterrent from dishonesty.

Prayer to close:

Forgive us, Holy Father, for not realizing how much the truth matters. Help us to be a people who love the truth as you love the truth. Work in us to rid our lives of any form of deceit. Create a hunger in us for the truth and let us daily go to the Word to be fed. Motivate us by your intense love. When someone we love is caught in sin, help us to love them, pray for them, and use the law and gospel in appropriate ways. Give us the heart of Jesus to do this well. In Jesus' name we pray. Amen.

CHAPTER 7

Figuring Out What Is and Isn't Our Business

Deliberately making others' business ours

Read 2 Samuel 11:1-26; 23:8,39.

It's often said we hurt those who are closest to us. When we realize Uriah was one of David's mighty men, a man who had risked his life with and for David on multiple occasions, we start to comprehend the depravity of David's actions.

David was not minding his business. In fact, he decidedly turned his attention to Uriah's business. To mind his business would have been as easy as turning away when he saw Bathsheba bathing. He had another opportunity to turn away when the servant told him she was married to Uriah. Instead, he relished the view, sent for her, and slept with her.

When we make other people's business our business, it often ends badly. I can't tell you the number of times I've been up in arms about something going on in a friend's life or with a family member or church member or a neighbor and my husband reminds me, "Amber, it's not your business."

So often we don't delineate where our business ends and the next person's business begins. If we hear about it, is it our business? If we see it, is it our business? How do we know? It is not by coincidence that things come to our attention. Often it is God's way of opening our eyes to a situation. But what do we do with that business once we know about it?

Shortly after I was married, my mother drove up to my house to hear me arguing with my new husband. The windows were open, and we weren't being quiet about our differences. After a few minutes, my mom backed out of the driveway and went home, praying for our marriage and, more importantly, our hearts. She didn't tell me about the incident for several years. During those first years of marriage when I called her because I was upset at my husband, she defended the marriage, not her daughter.

Many times I invited my mother to make my marriage her business. My godly mother recognized the importance of staying outside the marriage while supporting, praying for, and guiding me. Knowing something does not give you permission to act, give your opinion, or choose a side. Sometimes knowing is just an opportunity to pray for the parties involved.

It's becoming harder and harder to mind our business because social media brings everyone's business right to us. How do we discern what to do with information once it comes into our space? How do we decide if we should deal with the information at all? How much information on social media is useful, and how much is just a distraction from more important things?

If I'm honest, a good portion of my "friends" on social media are people I've only met once or twice. Some of my "friends" are friends of friends whom I've never met at all. Chances are slim that they'd want my advice or answers even if they were in a bind. Even the people I know well are often posting about people I don't know. More often than not, I turn my phone off after scrolling through social media, feeling as if I've thrown away time I can't recover.

One of the problems with being a busybody is that sometimes when we get into other people's business, our lives don't look as good. We start to compare, and their lives seem better. In John chapter 21, Peter wanted to know about John. Jesus told Peter not to worry about John. Peter needed to live his life, run his race, and do the work God had for him to do. If we concentrate on those things, we likely won't have time to be busybodies, and we might even find we are much more content.

Getting involved with Bathsheba led David to go to great lengths to cover his tracks. Had David turned away that evening on the roof and gone back to the palace, back to his wives and his children, he would have spared himself the consequences of his sin. Instead, covering up his sin became his new business.

The consequences to David's family were devastating. God told David the sword would not depart from his family. There will be consequences when we insist on getting into other people's business too. It may weaken a friendship, ostracize a neighbor, or cause friction between you and your adult children. If those words cause a little sting because you're living in those consequences now, let me remind you of what Nathan told David: "The LORD has taken away your sin" (2 Samuel 12:13).

I've been there too, and my guess is that I'll likely fall into it again because by nature I'm a take-charge kind of person. Learning to mind our business without the constant desire to look at or get involved in other people's business will serve us well and save us from those consequences.

For further consideration/discussion:

1. Not minding his business led David to covet Bathsheba. What things do you covet when you start paying attention to other people's business?

2. Ultimately, Uriah suffered the most from David's sin. How do our spouses and children suffer when we get involved in other people's business?

3. My husband and mother have guarded me from getting involved in things I need not be involved in. Who keeps you in check? How can you tactfully keep others from getting involved in situations they shouldn't be in?

The blessing of minding our business

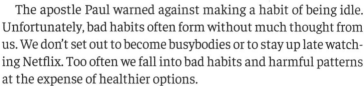

Read 1 Timothy 5:13-15.

The apostle Paul warned against making a habit of being idle. Unfortunately, bad habits often form without much thought from us. We don't set out to become busybodies or to stay up late watching Netflix. Too often we fall into bad habits and harmful patterns at the expense of healthier options.

While it's easy to fall into bad habits, good habits are usually by choice. Getting up to go to the gym doesn't just happen. Reading our Bible every day or going to church every week will happen when we make those things a priority.

The blessing of minding my business is taking care of the things right in front of me, things that get neglected if I'm wasting time or browsing through other people's business. When I look at my house and yard, I have no reason to waste time worrying about what other people are doing. When I think of all the ministry efforts I care about, I could stay busy for a long time. That's not taking into account the relationships I want to build with my spouse, children, Christian friends, and neighbors.

Paul's admonition is about managing our time in a way that glorifies God. It's a cure for the other sins I am prone to falling into too. Instead of worrying, I can scrub the floor and pray; instead of complaining, I can wash the dishes and thank God for my family; instead of envying, I can weed and pray God gives me a grateful heart to see how good he's been to me; and instead of doubting, I can go for a walk and pray God gives me courage to keep going. In all of this, I have a double blessing. Not only am I engaging in conversation with my heavenly Father throughout the day, but things are getting done too.

If I'm honest, sometimes I'm happy to avoid the to-do list because it's not fun or exciting. I *want* to be lazy. I *don't care* if I get anything done.

We all have days when we're feeling under the weather or less than productive. As a rule, if I allow myself to go there too often, I regret it. Why? Because inevitably someone will knock on the door, and I regret that my house isn't as clean as I'd want it to be. Or I let the house and yard go, and then it's time for a confirmation or graduation party or even just a holiday, and I'm scrambling to get done all the things I neglected.

When I keep up with things at home, I'm more likely to invite people into our home, and I'm more comfortable when they just show up. I want people to stop over if they're lonely or struggling or in need of advice. I don't want to hesitate, and I don't want to turn them away.

This has always been an area of struggle for me. Our house is notoriously lived in; so is our garage. Even our driveway is worse for wear thanks to years of people working on cars. When my son's friend drove up recently, he explained he had some work to do on his car. He started the project at his house, but his parents were annoyed at the noise and the mess. So in his words, he came to our house because he knew we wouldn't mind.

I don't want to clean my house or work in my yard till I have no time left to serve God or others. But I also don't want to spend my days lollygagging at the expense of doing meaningful work at home, in the church, and in the community.

Work is fulfilling, and there is always work to be done in our homes, at our jobs, at our church, or simply helping others. Wasted time on social media or in front of our TV or phone or computer often breeds discontent and leaves us unambitious and stirring up trouble.

Jesus said, "The harvest is plentiful but the workers are few. Ask the Lord of the harvest, therefore, to send out workers into his harvest field" (Matthew 9:37,38). When I remember that I am a worker in God's kingdom and that as long as I'm alive I'm God's hands and feet on earth, I'm more eager to work at what he's given me to do. As I'm working, I'm more likely to pray that God will use me and my house and my yard to serve him and his people well. I get it wrong far too often. I easily slip into distraction and idleness. But when I'm in the Word and as the Holy Spirit prompts, I get back to work in my home and in his kingdom.

For further consideration/discussion:

4. Being a good friend is being genuinely concerned. If we're strictly looking for information for the sake of talking about it, we're being a busybody. Looking to encourage or help someone is different. There's also a difference between seeking information in order to share it and checking in so we know how to pray. Sometimes a conversation goes sideways before we realize what's happening. How can we keep our conversations godly? How can we keep from being busybodies?

5. When are you most likely to waste time on social media?

6. How can you combat the temptation to waste time on things that don't deserve your time and energy?

7. Take a minute to really consider your goals. What deserves your time and energy more than social media or hours on Netflix or in front of the TV? What things can you do that would have spiritual value?

8. Have you ever looked up people on social media to spy on them? (Who hasn't?) You hear of an arrest or a failed marriage so you scroll through people's pages looking for clues. Or you go through their photos to see where things started to unravel. With social media this is so easy to do. What lessons should we take away from this?

You can be a busybody without being on social media. It's done over lunch or a phone call or when you purposely seek out someone in the know in order to get information. The question is, What are you doing with the information you get? Genuine concern will motivate you to call someone you haven't heard from in a while or knock on a neighbor's door. But if it's about seeking information to gossip, the apostle Paul would urge you to make better use of your time.

The exception: rescuing the lost

Read Ezekiel 3:16-21 and Matthew 18:15.

God draws a distinction we are not always willing to draw. There's minding our business, and then there's being afraid to step on someone's toes because they might not like us anymore. When it comes to sin, minding our business is not the best option.

There's good reason that God takes sin seriously. We like to think we'll all live to an old age. Many—if not most—of us take our faith for granted. We imagine there will be a time to get more serious about it; there will be a time we'll want to get to know God more.

Likewise, we tend to downplay our sin and idolatry. We become engrossed in acquiring more and easily fall into putting other things before Sunday worship. We watch things on TV we shouldn't. It's easy enough to justify. The plot is good, the acting terrific, and the special effects amazing.

Justifying sin dulls our conscience little by little. We let the devil and the world plant, water, and tend seeds of immorality. What seemed vulgar once upon a time slowly becomes normal. Every sin, when done enough without accountability or repentance, becomes commonplace.

I'm not sure I know anyone who likes confrontation, whether you're the one confronting or the one being confronted. It's far easier to just mind my business and put my blinders on to what others are doing. There's just one problem with that mentality: Satan is warring for souls. He doesn't want people to repent and turn from their sin. He certainly isn't cheering for anyone to have the fulfillment and fruitfulness that come from walking with God.

God, on the other hand, has a heart for the lost and straying. Jesus said,

> What do you think? If a man owns a hundred sheep, and one of them wanders away, will he not leave the ninety-nine on the hills and go to look for the one that wandered off? And if he finds it, truly I tell you, he is happier about that one sheep than about the ninety-nine that did not wander off. In the same way your Father in heaven is not willing that any of these little ones should perish. (Matthew 18:12-14)

The apostle Paul urged Timothy to pray for all people because God "wants all people to be saved and to come to a knowledge of the truth" (1 Timothy 2:4). Those kingdom workers Jesus said were in short supply are you and me. The fields are ripe!

Why are we not concerned for people who were once part of our fellowship but are now going down the path of sin and walking away from God and the church? Why don't we care when our loved ones are swallowed by the deceitfulness of the world, when their only concern is the amount of money they make, climbing the corporate ladder, or making sure their children excel at sports at the expense of going to church? If we don't say something, who will?

God made it clear to Ezekiel: If you don't tell them, I'll hold you accountable. That's a frightening thought. British pastor Charles Spurgeon put it this way: "God save us from living in comfort while sinners are sinking into hell."[13] We have the truth. We dare not mind our business at the expense of people's salvation. If they don't listen, then at least we've tried.

More than once I've told someone the truth of God's Word only to be rejected. Years later I've seen those same people either at a point of wanting to know the truth or sometimes even living as Christians. The initial rejection was only part of the story. The apostle Paul said, "I planted the seed, Apollos watered it, but God has been making it grow. So neither the one who plants nor the one who waters is anything, but only God, who makes things grow" (1 Corinthians 3:6,7).

---

[13] Charles Spurgeon, *The Complete Works of C. H. Spurgeon*, Vol. 83 (Harrington, DE: Delmarva Publications, Inc., 2015), p. 102.

Our little seed may not amount to much. Maybe we just invited the grandkids to VBS. Maybe we just asked our nieces and nephews to come to the church picnic. Maybe we sent a podcast or devotion to our sister or brother or friend. Don't get discouraged if you don't see fruit. Be patient and keep praying! The little seed we planted may seem insignificant, but God can use it to work in ways we might never see.

For further consideration/discussion:

9. We all have people in our lives we know are straying. Write down a list of people in your life who are or have wandered from the truth. What has kept you from talking to them about their choices?

10. When is the last time you made contact with these people? Consider inviting them for dinner or to take a walk. Send them a text or call them up. Listen to their heart, and as God allows, put nuggets of truth in the conversation. Write the names you wrote down for question 9. Next to each name, put your action plan. Do you plan to invite them to dinner, send a card, or just pray for now?

11. Now make a list of unbelievers you know from the people you work with, neighbors you enjoy talking to, or even the ones who've made your life miserable. Consider Spurgeon's words and choose the name of one person you want to contact in the next month just for the sake of showing kindness and opening a door. Circle that name and start praying for God to prepare that person's heart!

Key takeaways:

+ Knowing information doesn't mean we need to be involved in the situation. Often, it is merely a chance for us to pray for God to intervene and work things out.

+ Stay busy doing what God puts in front of you while being alert for opportunities to encourage and pray for others. And while you work, pray, listen to the Bible or a Christian podcast, and worship!

✝ Being idle often leads to collecting data on others. Never has that been easier than when we scroll social media. A quick scroll can keep you informed of those who need prayers, but if you're scrolling because you're bored and looking at the same posts you saw two hours earlier, it may be time to do something else!

✝ Jesus clearly shows we are to walk our walk without needing to know or understand the plans God has for someone else.

✝ When our friends and loved ones are falling away from God, we can lovingly encourage them to return to the Lord. We can't assume that someone else will do it or that it isn't our business.

✝ Even when we don't see change in the hearts and lives of loved ones, we can continue to pray that God works faith in their hearts.

Prayer to close:

Heavenly Father, you call us to be good stewards of everything you give us. Forgive us for squandering our opportunities. Forgive us for seeking information we don't need to know. Give us discernment to use our mouth and time in ways that honor you. In Jesus' name we pray. Amen.

CHAPTER 8
The Heart
Behind Complaining

Fear-driven complaining

Read Numbers 13:26–14:11.

Imagine what our ancestors would think if they could see us. Machines wash and dry our clothes, cut our lawns, and blow snow from our driveways. Boxes entertain us. Handheld devices give us information and recipes on demand. We have food readily available and access to running water. We travel in heated cars. We have doctors, medicine, and hospitals a few minutes away. If our ancestors were to look at our lives, no doubt they would think that we'd be constantly full of happiness as we enjoy our seemingly simple lives.

Likewise, Moses and Aaron brought the people to the edge of an exceedingly wonderful land. The produce was abundant. The cities were built. God had promised the Israelites it would be theirs. You would think the people would be ecstatic. But the people weren't happy. In fact, they were miserable. What was the problem?

In a word: fear.

Fear kept ten of the spies from trusting God's promises. Fear kept the Israelites from believing that God, who had rescued them from the Egyptians, would rescue them from this people. Fear led to discouragement, which led to rebellion and the people wanting to return to Egypt.

Two of the spies were different. Joshua and Caleb saw the land, and instead of being afraid, they realized God was big enough to conquer the land. They also recognized that the main problem was fear. They said,

> The land we passed through and explored is exceedingly good. If the LORD is pleased with us, he will lead us into that land, a land flowing with milk and honey, and will give it to us. Only do not rebel against the LORD. And do not be afraid of the people of the land, because we will devour them. Their protection is gone, but the LORD is with us. Do not be afraid of them. (Numbers 14:7-9)

How many of our complaints originate out of a place of fear? When the COVID-19 global pandemic arrived in March 2020, I struggled with debilitating fear. My husband was a nurse on the hospital floor designated to care for COVID-19 patients in our community. I was a wreck for a solid month. I devoured news stories and stocked up on food and toiletries. I "mother-henned" my children. I didn't see how we would survive. Eventually, through time in the Word with some mature Christian friends, prayer, and turning off the news, I came to accept the situation as out of my control. I prayed for the Lord's protection. Rather than live in constant worry, I came to understand God was bigger than COVID-19.

In Psalm 27, David resolutely determined fear had no place in his life. He had plenty of enemies and life-threatening situations, but his confidence was in the Lord.

> ' The LORD is my light and my salvation—
>   whom shall I fear?
> The LORD is the stronghold of my life—
>   of whom shall I be afraid?
> When the wicked advance against me
>   to devour me,
> it is my enemies and my foes
>   who will stumble and fall.
> Though an army besiege me,
>   my heart will not fear;

> though war break out against me,
> even then I will be confident. (verses 1-3)

What a contrast to the Israelites at the border of Canaan! They gave in to their fear and refused to be persuaded that God would give them what he had promised. If David had succumbed to fear, he would have sat on the hills with the rest of the army of Israel instead of facing Goliath. He never would have gone to war. Because he put fear aside and put his confidence in God, he consistently went to war and expanded Israel's borders.

The disciples also complained out of fear. When the sea turned ferocious and the situation became more than they could handle, they went to Jesus with an accusation: "Don't you care if we drown?" (Mark 4:38). After calming the sea, Jesus chided the disciples for their lack of faith. Does that mean we can face the terrifying situations in our life with faith? And how does one get this faith?

Faith doesn't mean that we have no fear, only that we act in spite of it. The apostle Paul told the Corinthians, "I came to you in weakness with great fear and trembling" (1 Corinthians 2:3). That seems a strange thing for the apostle Paul to say. Hadn't he gone from city to city preaching with might and power? A quick read through Acts chapters 14-16 shows that going from city to city often resulted in being beaten, stoned, left for dead, flogged, and put in prison. Knowing what may come didn't keep him from his important work. *Despite* his fear, he pressed on.

If fear dictates our actions, we, like the Israelites, may find our efforts are used up by complaining about our impossible situations. We can't control our circumstances, so the solution has to be in our response to the circumstances. Fear will come, but will it lead us to complain and refuse to go on, or will our fear drive us to seek God and put our faith in him?

Courage is a matter of perspective. A popular meme puts it this way: "Don't tell God how big the storm is. Tell the storm how big your God is." See the difference? As long as we look at the storm, everything seems impossible. When we fix our eyes on God, we know he will work for our good and easily do the impossible.

God knew our tendency would be to see the circumstances instead of him. That's why Scripture comforts us over and over:

- Deuteronomy 31:8—"The LORD himself goes before you and will be with you; he will never leave you nor forsake you. Do not be afraid; do not be discouraged."

- Joshua 1:9—"Have I not commanded you? Be strong and courageous. Do not be afraid; do not be discouraged, for the LORD your God will be with you wherever you go."

- Isaiah 41:10—"Do not fear, for I am with you; do not be dismayed, for I am your God. I will strengthen you and help you; I will uphold you with my righteous right hand."

- Jeremiah 51:46—"Do not lose heart or be afraid when rumors are heard in the land; one rumor comes this year, another the next, rumors of violence in the land and of ruler against ruler."

- Matthew 10:31—"Don't be afraid; you are worth more than many sparrows."

- Matthew 14:27—"Jesus immediately said to them: 'Take courage! It is I. Don't be afraid.'"

Fear will always be part of our lives. We will find ourselves from time to time in situations that are impossible for us to overcome. Those are the moments we go back to Scripture and the assurance that "nothing is impossible with God" (Luke 1:37 NIV 1984). God delights at our invitation to walk into our impossible situations. He was intimately involved in his people's lives all throughout Scripture. Why would he care less about us?

God doesn't want us to live in fear. We can face the things that frighten us not with complaints but with a steadfast resolve to bring the situation to God and rely on him to give us the courage, strength, and wisdom to get through the storms.

For further consideration/discussion:
1. Look at the difference in how the spies talked to the people and Moses (Numbers 13:31–14:4) and how David talked about God in Psalm 27. Then compare the disciples' accusation

against Jesus in the boat to how David talked to God. How will your prayers change when they are driven by fear compared to when they are driven by trust in an all-powerful God?

2. Fear boils down to unbelief. The spies didn't believe God would give them the land. How do we make sure fear isn't undermining our actions?

3. Look at Numbers 14:11. How does God feel when we choose to complain rather than trust him?

Entitlement-driven complaining

Read 2 Kings 5:1-14.

God gave us incredible insight through the descriptions he used in the Bible. Naaman clearly was an important man by worldly standards. He was "commander of the army," a "great man," "highly regarded," a "valiant soldier." These things would lead most people to think highly of themselves. The details, however, leave little reason for Naaman to be arrogant: "through him the LORD had given victory to Aram" (verse 1). God enabled Naaman to win, made him a strong soldier and leader, and gave him his position of authority.

But the fact that Naaman's prominence was from God escaped him. When Naaman set out for Israel, he brought a significant amount of money and ten sets of clothes. If someone didn't know his importance before seeing his caravan, perhaps the clothes and treasure chests would clue the person in. If anyone deserved to be healed, certainly Naaman did.

The king of Israel's complaints at Naaman's arrival stemmed from fear. Aram had been pillaging Israel's people and stealing their children. Not long before, King Ahab had been wounded and killed while in battle against Aram (1 Kings 22). Now a commander of the army arrived requesting healing. For an unbelieving king, it seemed another provocation.

Elisha wasn't impressed by social standing or the amount of gold Naaman possessed. In fact, he didn't give Naaman the satisfaction of noticing. He was unconcerned with worldly status, fame, or an elevated sense of importance and didn't go out to see all that Naaman possessed.

Naaman expected VIP treatment. He certainly wasn't interested in what seemed to be foolish instructions delivered by a servant. He was, after all, a man of high standing with more than enough money. How dare he be told to dip in a dirty river?

Money doesn't earn God's favor. Social standing doesn't factor into God answering our prayers. In fact, it was the simple faith of the servants that prompted Naaman to believe and act in faith.

My sense of entitlement leads to a lot of complaining too. I take credit when God works through me, thinking I somehow have rank in God's kingdom. At times I've viewed being a lifelong Christian as a status symbol, as if I were somehow better than those who are still blinded from the truth. I slip into thinking my time is more valuable than another's, which leads to impatience. I can spew a tirade of complaints toward the person who didn't perform to my expectations and do things my way.

Any good works we do are as useless as the money and clothes in Naaman's chariot. We can't earn God's grace. All of us stand before God as equals: equally steeped in sin, equally in need of a Savior, and equally having access to the saving grace of Jesus.

The apostle Paul explained,

> In your relationships with one another, have the same mindset as Christ Jesus: Who, being in very nature God, did not consider equality with God something to be used to his own advantage; rather, he made himself nothing by taking the very nature of a servant, being made in human

likeness. And being found in appearance as a man, he humbled himself by becoming obedient to death—even death on a cross! (Philippians 2:5-8)

Jesus had every reason to feel entitled, and he gave that up to walk the earth as a human so that he could take our trouble on himself. But there's more! He didn't leave heaven just to rule and reign on earth. He left his due honor and glory to carry out our death sentence, which included a cruel crucifixion reserved for the worst criminals—us!

Why do I think I should get preferential treatment? Why should I be served first or get what I want all the time? Why should traffic get out of my way when I'm late for work? Why should I expect the neighbors to do things my way or the school district to do what is best for me or my household to run to my expectations?

Naaman might have walked away to die as a leper if he hadn't been convinced to put his entitlement aside. We don't want to waste our time squabbling about who should serve whom or whose turn it is to do that chore. We've got people to serve and gospel seeds to plant.

Martin Luther said, "Where the heart is right with God and this [first] commandment is kept, fulfillment of all the others will follow of its own accord."[14] That is to say, as I love God and realize what he has done for me and as I understand the humility of Christ, I'm naturally going to love others more, recognizing that they too are people Jesus died to save.

For further consideration/discussion:

4. Is complaining your go-to response when things don't go your way? How does that indicate a sense of entitlement brooding in your heart?

---

[14] Large Catechism, Part I:48, *The Book of Concord: The Confessions of the Evangelical Lutheran Church*, translated and edited by Theodore G. Tappert (Philadelphia: Fortress Press, 1959), p. 371, quoted in Leroy Dobberstein, *Law and Gospel: Bad News—Good News*, of The People's Bible Teachings series (Milwaukee: Northwestern Publishing House, 1973), p. 157.

5. In the gospels Jesus shows he was completely in tune to his Father's will. Jesus didn't demand his way. In fact, on multiple occasions he reminded his disciples that he came to serve. In what areas of your life have you demanded your way? How would things change if you acquired a heart of servitude rather than entitlement?

6. Jesus told his disciples that when he returns to judge the nations on judgment day, he will remind his followers that they took care of him when he was sick, visited him when he was in prison, and fed him when he was hungry. Read Matthew 25:40. How does this change your attitude about serving people you otherwise might not feel obligated to serve?

Acquiring the attitude of Christ

Read Luke 10:38-42.

Much has been said about this account. Martha complained. Mary sat at Jesus' feet. Mary knew what Martha missed. As we soak in the Word, we can't help but become more humble, more ready to serve, and less eager to complain. We'll spend less time comparing and a whole lot more time basking in the fact that we are forgiven children of God. It wasn't that Mary didn't want to help. It was that Martha was scurrying at the wrong time. Yes, a meal needed to be made. That could happen after Jesus finished teaching. No doubt, Mary would have happily helped her sister then.

We can't stop complaining of our own volition. Try as we might, our old Adam loves to complain. We need a battle plan that is not dependent on our human frailty. It starts by sitting at Jesus' feet like Mary.

Dwight D. Eisenhower said, "In preparing for battle I have always found that plans are useless, but planning is indispensable."[15] Christians are active participants in a war between the kingdom of God and the kingdom of evil. Eisenhower more or less said it will never play out exactly as you imagine, but in your daily preparation, you are preparing to meet any challenge. The apostle Paul said, "Our struggle is not against flesh and blood, but against the rulers, against the authorities, against the powers of this dark world and against the spiritual forces of evil in the heavenly realms" (Ephesians 6:12).

Satan would so much rather we complain than praise. He'd rather we keep score than serve joyfully. He'd rather we think God has abandoned us than believe he's with us. In order to meet the temptation to complain, we need to be armed. Rarely can we plan for specific circumstances, but by being in the Word, we can prepare our hearts to have an attitude of service, gratitude, and contentment no matter comes our way.

The devil is a grumbler. In the Garden of Eden, he incited Eve to discontent. He tempted Jesus and hoped for the same outcome. Jesus didn't fall for Satan's schemes the way Eve did. He knew who his Father was and that God loved him and was in control.

If we are going to keep Satan at bay, we need to remember who God is. When we're afraid, we need to remember our Father is the almighty God. He created the heavens and the earth. He gave us life and preserves us until the moment he determines it's time to go home.

Consider a little girl who is afraid to jump from one stone to the next to cross a river. Her father reaches to hold his child's hand and says, "Trust me. I won't let you fall." What does that child do? She grabs her father's hand and walks across the river with her father.

When we're overwhelmed like Martha with all we have to do, we need eternal perspective. Are we obsessing over details that don't ultimately matter? Is it worth stressing for two weeks to put together the perfect Christmas gathering, or would you rather be worry-free with a simpler Christmas while making time each day for prayer and Bible reading?

---

[15] Oxford Reference, https://www.oxfordreference.com/view/10.1093/acref/9780191826719.001.0001/q-oro-ed4-00004005 (accessed 2023).

When I remember who God is (my heavenly Father who loves me) and that God is in control (able to do anything), why wouldn't I trust him? When I remember what Jesus was willing to do (come to earth to die in my place), why wouldn't I want to serve others the way Jesus served me? Looking at all I've been given, don't I joyfully want to use what I have for the benefit of others? Keeping these basic truths in front of me gives me fewer reasons to complain.

Jesus used the Word to fight Satan's temptations. As we read God's Word, we are reminded that God loves us unconditionally and is in control. If God was with Abraham, Jacob, Joseph, Gideon, Ruth, Esther, Hezekiah, and so many others, surely he will be with us. If we're in a prison, as Joseph was, God will make sure we know he is there too. If we suffer for standing up for God, we can be assured the angel is with us just as he was in the fire with Shadrach, Meshach, and Abednego. And when the situation seems dire, with no hope for success, we need only remember that God directed the pebble that left David's slingshot and killed the giant.

First John 5:14 says, "This is the confidence we have in approaching God: that if we ask anything according to his will, he hears us." When we're overwhelmed, afraid, and feeling like we're being treated poorly, we have a choice. We can complain, but that's not likely to change anything. Or we can pray and invite God to work in and through the situation.

Jesus had good reason to complain while hanging from the cross. He was there for our sins, not his, and in excruciating pain. Instead of muttering, he asked his Father to forgive the men who put him there.

Rarely do we understand everything that's going on when we complain. God has given us so much. He's worked mightily in our lives over and over. And over and over our words treat him with contempt rather than giving him the thanksgiving he deserves. May we, like the hymn writer, learn to say:

> What a friend we have in Jesus,
> All our sins and griefs to bear!
> What a privilege to carry
> Ev'rything to God in prayer!

Oh, what peace we often forfeit,
Oh, what needless pain we bear,
All because we do not carry
Ev'rything to God in prayer! (CW 720:1)

For further consideration/discussion:
7. We often face very real and serious needs. What emotions, other than fear and entitlement, contribute to our responses when we complain?

8. Name some exaggerations we often use in our complaints when we are desperate for something.

9. Complaining clouds our spiritual view, shrouds our perspective, and has us looking to others for help. Often, we aren't even looking for help; we are simply bemoaning our circumstances. How can we stop this vicious and useless cycle?

Key takeaways:
+ Uncontrolled fear is behind a lot of our complaints.

+ Instead of us looking at our circumstances, they should prayerfully drive us to look to God.

+ Sometimes we complain because we feel we're entitled, thinking we deserve better circumstances or treatment.

+ Jesus had every reason to feel entitled, but he humbled himself completely and served us.

✝ God's Word reminds us that God loves us and is in control.

✝ Satan is a grumbler. Jesus trusted and served. Christians want to be on team Jesus, worshiping and praising God whatever comes our way.

✝ Heaven is where we'll have perfect circumstances and perfect peace.

Prayer to close:

Lord, forgive us for the many times we have chosen to complain instead of turning to you. Your Word reveals how much you love your people and want to be their refuge and aid. Teach us to honor you by refusing to complain. Instead, help us to call on you and glorify you. In Jesus' name we pray. Amen.

CHAPTER 9
Comparison Kills

Comparing our blessings to others

Read Luke 12:13-34.

Comparison is perhaps the easiest way to fall into discontent. It happened to my husband and me when we were a young married couple and we watched our friends buy houses. Then as they had children, they bought bigger houses and newer vehicles. They went on vacations.

My husband was still in college when we got married, and when he graduated, we had a baby. I cut down my hours at work. We didn't have the same budget as our friends who continued to have two full-time incomes. It didn't take long for us to realize we had to learn to be content, or we'd be very unhappy.

Our journey to contentment started by identifying where we placed value. Would we value time more than money? Did we crave things or experiences? Did I want to be a hands-on part of my children's learning activities or entrust them to someone else?

Possessions can be an amazing blessing, but Jesus said life does not consist in the abundance of our possessions. All too often we dwell on what we don't have. If I'm longingly looking at all you have while noting the absence of the same things in my life, I tend to be discontent. Some of the most content people I know don't have an abundance of physical things. Instead, they have and appreciate blessings that can't be bought—a good marriage, loving family, faithful Christian friends, and peace with God.

In fact, not having everything we want can be a blessing. All things require maintenance and energy and time. We have to make choices. If we buy everything now to keep up with our neighbors and friends, we may not have money to put away for retirement. That may keep us working longer while others retire. Or we may work less and have more time to spend with family but less money to buy a newer vehicle or go on vacation. Rarely will we have it all.

No retirement fund can offer true security. Money can't keep us healthy. It can't keep us from devastating circumstances. There's no security apart from the grace (undeserved love) and mercy (withholding of judgment) of God. Day by day, God gives us what we need, in good health or bad, in poverty or excess, usually without us even realizing it.

The things of this world quickly lose value and fall into disrepair. The fads and must-haves of one season are of little value the next. If we insist on comparing, someone will always have more.

Jesus suggested that instead of worrying about what we have on earth, we should concentrate on storing up treasures in heaven. He's asking us to invest our time, money, and energy into bringing souls into the kingdom of God. Those the Spirit brings to faith through our efforts and as a result of our gifts will be in heaven for eternity.

In Luke chapter 16, Jesus compared a rich man who enjoyed all the pleasures of earth to a poor, sickly beggar, Lazarus, who sat at his gate. Both men eventually died, and their earthly status disappeared. The rich man's riches didn't buy him a place in heaven. He went to hell and everlasting torment. The poor beggar went to heaven, where he no longer experienced the pain and hunger that he endured on earth. Comparatively, Lazarus won.

Our human nature drifts easily into working for earthly pleasure at the expense of heavenly treasure. Being in the Word and with our Christian friends will help us keep an eternal perspective. The Word and our accountability partners will remind us that our sorrows and troubles on earth are not even worth thinking about in view of the glory and joys of heaven.

Comparisons and unfulfilled expectations can leave us miserable. If we're not married by a certain age, if we don't get the job we thought we deserved, if our husband doesn't turn out to be the Prince Charming we wanted, we can be left devastated. Our false expectations come from the idea that we can control our lives. When we concede that we have relatively little control over anything and surrender to God's will, we—with the strength God provides—can take the joys and the sorrows of life in stride.

For further consideration/discussion:
1. In Luke 12:15, what was Jesus' initial warning to the man who asked for help with his brother regarding the inheritance?

2. What are the blessings of not having everything we want?

3. Jesus said, "Where your treasure is, there your heart will be also" (Matthew 6:21). In an ideal world, what would you treasure? What would you make time to do each day? How can you make that happen?

Comparing talents and abilities

Read Psalm 139:14 and Ephesians 2:10.

I wish these passages hung in every home and were explained to every child. Imagine how much less angst we'd have if we only understood these important words.

Psalm 139:14 assures with absolute certainty that you are not an afterthought. God designed you. God intentionally designed you with all the talents and traits and abilities he thought you should have. Being fierce or shy, energetic or calm, driven or tenderhearted is no mistake. God created you the way you are for his purpose.

Ephesians 2:10 says that he created you in Christ to do the works he has planned for you. That good work may be caring for infant children. That good work may be giving your ear to a troubled coworker. That good work may be leading your children in prayer. Take a moment to think of the many things you have done today that God prepared you to do.

Don't get me wrong. We can screw this up. The wrong influences can convince us to be boisterous, demanding, and unapologetic. That's us going our own way and refusing to take God's Word to heart. Here's how we get it right. When we, through examination and what the apostle Paul referred to as "sober judgment," find our unique talents, we can use them to God's glory in God's kingdom.

I didn't know that I could teach. It never occurred to me to try. When the staff minister at my church asked me to teach my daughter's Sunday school class, I told him I wasn't a teacher. He assured me I didn't need to be and gave me the materials to walk me through the lessons. A short while later my pastor suggested I teach the mom's Bible study I wanted to start. I did my best impression of Moses at the burning bush, but my pastor didn't take my excuses any better than God took Moses' excuses.

It didn't take long for me to realize I loved teaching. Sometimes others have to show us what we don't see in ourselves. It's not worth comparing ourselves to anyone else because, as Paul explains, we all have different functions to make the church whole.

> Just as a body, though one, has many parts, but all its many parts form one body, so it is with Christ. For we were all baptized by one Spirit so as to form one body— whether Jews or Gentiles, slave or free—and we were all given the one Spirit to drink. Even so the body is not made up of one part but of many.
> Now if the foot should say, "Because I am not a hand, I do not belong to the body," it would not for that reason stop being part of the body. And if the ear should say,

"Because I am not an eye, I do not belong to the body,"
it would not for that reason stop being part of the body.
If the whole body were an eye, where would the sense of
hearing be? If the whole body were an ear, where would
the sense of smell be? But in fact God has placed the
parts in the body, every one of them, just as he wanted
them to be. If they were all one part, where would the
body be? As it is, there are many parts, but one body.
The eye cannot say to the hand, "I don't need you!" And
the head cannot say to the feet, "I don't need you!" On
the contrary, those parts of the body that seem to be
weaker are indispensable, and the parts that we think
are less honorable we treat with special honor. And the
parts that are unpresentable are treated with special
modesty, while our presentable parts need no special
treatment. But God has put the body together, giving
greater honor to the parts that lacked it, so that there
should be no division in the body, but that its parts
should have equal concern for each other. If one part
suffers, every part suffers with it; if one part is honored,
every part rejoices with it. (1 Corinthians 12:12-26)

Satan would love for us to spend our days obsessing about what
we don't have. We can look at the way a woman leads and wonder
why we weren't given that gift. When the pastor publicly thanks her
for using her gift, we can dig a pit of despair with a shovel of insecurity. Or we can rejoice that she used her gift; we can be spurred
on "toward love and good deeds" (Hebrews 10:24). The apostle Paul
says, "If one part is honored, every part rejoices with it." When one
uses a gift, we all benefit.

I've learned from experience that hospitality is not my gift. When
I put something in the oven, it has a 50-50 chance of being edible.
It has a 90 percent chance of not looking like anything special. If
forced, I could decorate or sew, but it would not look like something
produced by someone with gifts in those areas. I marvel at those
who have different gifts than I do, but I no longer worry about not
having those same gifts.

I was created for a purpose, and you were created for a different purpose. We don't have to step on each other's feet. We can recognize how God gifted us and do the work he has for us to our fullest potential and for his glory.

For further consideration/discussion:

4. How did God gift you spiritually? Can you lead, teach, encourage, or serve? Are you the first person to open your home and make a meal for someone? Do you visit the people in the nursing home or hospital? Are you generous, funding projects behind the scenes?

5. Sometimes we struggle to use our gifts because we don't know what they are. Spiritual gift inventories are great ways to learn how you are gifted. If you've never filled one out, you can find free inventories online. Not only will they help you discover what your gifts are, but they also will help you to see how you are not gifted. Why is that important?

6. What has hindered you from service in the kingdom of God?

The trouble with comparing sins

Read John 8:1-11.

In your prayers, how often haven't you brought someone to God the way the teachers of the law and the Pharisees brought this woman? *Do you see what they've done, Lord? Can you tolerate such grievous sin?* Of course, there's nothing wrong with such a prayer when injustice is committed. When lives have been shattered and undue suffering has occurred at the hands of cruel people, how could we not bring it before our heavenly Father?

That, however, was not at the heart of the action of the teachers of the law and the Pharisees. They approached Jesus with what appeared to be a genuine question, but the Holy Spirit revealed through John their true intent. They hoped to trap Jesus in his words.

As much as I hate to admit it, my prayers too have been spoken with ill intent at times. On occasion, I have reminded God how awful the other person was as a way of justifying my own less-than-godly words and actions. *I shouldn't have lost my temper, I know, Lord, but do you see what I'm up against?*

It's amazing how easy it is to see every miniscule fault of others while missing our own behemoth sins. Jesus admonished: "Why do you look at the speck of sawdust in your brother's eye and pay no attention to the plank in your own eye? How can you say to your brother, 'Let me take the speck out of your eye,' when all the time there is a plank in your own eye? You hypocrite, first take the plank out of your own eye, and then you will see clearly to remove the speck from your brother's eye" (Matthew 7:3-5).

When we compare sins, all too often we rate the sins of others on a scale of our own making as a means of determining if their sins are worse or better than our own sins. Maybe I overeat or exaggerate the truth, but I don't use drugs or drive recklessly. It was exactly this sort of comparing that led Jesus to confront with conviction: Whoever is without sin, let him throw the first stone.

He addressed the issue again with the parable of the tax collector and the Pharisee in Luke chapter 18. Jesus told the parable to "some who were confident of their own righteousness and looked down on everyone else" (Luke 18:9). He said,

> Two men went up to the temple to pray, one a Pharisee and the other a tax collector. The Pharisee stood by himself and prayed: "God, I thank you that I am not like other people—robbers, evildoers, adulterers—or even like this tax collector. I fast twice a week and give a tenth of all I get." But the tax collector stood at a distance. He would

not even look up to heaven, but beat his breast and said, "God, have mercy on me, a sinner." (Luke 18:10-13)

Puritan William Plummer said concerning the Pharisee in this parable, "He glances at God but contemplates himself."[16] And isn't it easy to do! *God, I'm on the altar committee, I teach Sunday school, and I'm at church more than so-and-so—and definitely more than she.* If our works earned salvation, then it would be imperative to make sure God kept an accurate tally.

But Jesus said the tax collector, not the Pharisee, went home justified—the tax collector who found no worth in his own deeds and instead looked to God for mercy. That is how we become right with God.

Instead of comparing our sins to the sins of others, Jesus asks us to consider the spiritual depths of the commandments. Jesus asks us to examine the motives of *our* hearts and minds. He said, "You have heard that it was said to the people long ago, 'You shall not murder, and anyone who murders will be subject to judgment.' But I tell you that anyone who is angry with a brother or sister will be subject to judgment. You have heard that it was said, 'You shall not commit adultery.' But I tell you that anyone who looks at a woman lustfully has already committed adultery with her in his heart" (Matthew 5:21,22,27,28). We may convince ourselves that we're pretty good if we look at the commandments superficially. When we look at the commandments in light of the Word or the perfect life of Jesus, it's clear we "all have sinned and fall short of the glory of God" (Romans 3:23).

Unless you are praying and grieving over a fallen brother's or sister's choices or an unbeliever's stubborn refusal to see the truth, ruminating on another's sin is not the best use of your time. It's a great way to ruin a relationship. Our children don't want us following them around announcing their shortcomings, and neither do our spouses or parents or friends. There is a place for confrontation, and there are certainly times to hold our loved ones accountable, but it shouldn't be constant. Instead, we should make

---

[16] David McLemore, "The Parable of the Pharisee and the Tax Collector," Things of the Sort, https://www.thingsofthesort.com/bible-studies/2017/11/27/the-parable-of-the-pharisee-and-the-tax-collector.

sure our loved ones know they are forgiven and loved. Grace, not law, motivates a sanctified life. Christ's forgiveness will do what condemnation never will.

Christian comedian Mark Lowry said, "I ain't got time to hate your sin. Hate your own sin. Hating my sin is a full-time job.... You hate your sin. I'll hate my sin and let's love each other."[17]

For further consideration/discussion:

7. Whose sins are you most likely to compare to your own? Is it a spouse whose shortcomings drive you crazy, a coworker whose political view is different from yours, or maybe a sibling who doesn't carry his or her weight in caring for aging parents?

8. When you look at your sins, do you tend to think like the Pharisee or do you worry because you're afraid your sins may be too big to be covered by God's grace? What's the problem with either mentality?

9. In 2014, I attended a mom's conference and heard Gary Chapman, author of *The Five Love Languages*, speak. He said that in his experience counseling married couples, most people are able to identify a long list of faults in their spouse but can rarely see more than three faults of their own. Jesus asked us to take the plank out of our eye before attempting to help others overcome their own faults. With that in mind, make a list of five sins you struggle with. If you can't think of five, consider asking your spouse or your children or a coworker. Once you identify the sins, you can be more cognizant of them and work on them.

---

[17] Mark Lowry, "Becoming a recovering fundamentalist," https://www.youtube.com/watch?v=z2aeDPsrAaQ.

Key takeaways:

+ As Christians following Christ, we shouldn't worry about fitting in.

+ Jesus reminds us that worldly possessions lose their value; our efforts are best spent on eternal efforts.

+ The Holy Spirit has given each of us gifts to be used in his kingdom.

+ We easily lose our joy and opportunities for service if we compare our gifts to someone else's and think ours have little worth.

+ It's pleasing to God when we use our gifts to our full potential without worrying about what anyone else is doing.

+ Our first efforts should be to identify and work on our own sin instead of concentrating on the sinful tendencies of others.

+ All sin is despicable before God and equally covered by God's grace.

+ At times, we must lovingly go to friends or relatives to confront them about a sin that is affecting us and others. That should be the exception. The rule should be to remind people often that they are loved and forgiven.

Prayer to close:

Where the world has put hooks in my soul, release me, Lord. Help me desire you and you alone. Let me be willing to forsake all the world offers for the sake of the gospel. Holy Spirit, kindle in me the flame of faith, and spur me on to love and good deeds. Too often I have condemned the rest of the world while overlooking my own sin. Let me first and foremost be concerned with my own faults. Show me when I must confront others for their sins and when you would have me overlook them. Use me to rescue others from a meaningless way of life. Let your grace dictate my actions now and always. Jesus, in your holy name I pray. Amen.

CHAPTER 10

Manipulating to Run the Show

Manipulating people

Read Mark 6:17-29.

The saying goes, If Mama ain't happy, ain't nobody happy. Maybe it's true that women show their emotions more than men but, ideally, we don't want to use our emotions, particularly the negative ones, to ruin the mood of the house or workplace or church. Using subtle, manipulative words and actions to railroad someone who doesn't see things our way isn't God's way, and we can all be thankful for that!

Mark tells us Herod's wife was behind John the Baptist's arrest. She wanted John dead, but unfortunately for her, Herod had a righteous fear of John and didn't want to kill him. Herodias didn't care about her husband's fear of John. Herodias waited, and when the opportunity presented itself, she took advantage of her husband, his foolish promise, and his guests. She manipulated Herod, and John's head was delivered to her on a platter.

Her actions caused great distress to her husband. Another day, in a different situation, he might have refused her request, but because he had made a foolish promise in front of so many, he felt trapped. He wasn't, of course, but his pride kept him from admitting his foolish mistake.

Plenty of situations put us at odds with our husband, our pastor, or another person in authority. How are we going to act?

Manipulation doesn't care about relationships or reputations. It is simply a means to getting our ends by conniving or being passive-aggressive or pouting till we get what we want.

Herodias' daughter used her sexuality to manipulate Herod. Women learn from an early age that dressing a certain way and putting time into looks bring attention, and attention can lead to power. Proverbs 31:30 warns, "Charm is deceptive, and beauty is fleeting, but a woman who fears the LORD is to be praised." A woman of God doesn't use charm and beauty to deceive. The apostle Peter instructs, "Your beauty should not come from outward adornment, such as elaborate hairstyles and the wearing of gold jewelry or fine clothes" (1 Peter 3:3). The world tells us to put time and money into a seductive hairstyle, use clothes to accentuate our feminine curves, and show enough skin to pique men's interest.

It's not a sin to be beautiful, wear makeup, or want to look your best. The sin is using your beauty to illicit lust in order to get your way. Solomon warns that women like this are a trap: "In the end she is bitter as gall, sharp as a double-edged sword. Her feet go down to death; her steps lead straight to the grave" (Proverbs 5:4,5).

Herod would have done well to take Solomon's warning. Like the simple man described below in the words of Proverbs chapter 7, Herod allowed his stepdaughter to lure him. His eyes lusted, and "he followed her like an ox going to the slaughter, like a deer stepping into a noose till an arrow pierces his liver, like a bird darting into a snare, little knowing it will cost him his life" (Proverbs 7:22,23). Herod didn't die physically as a result of his actions, but spiritually he committed a grievous crime. He killed the Lord's prophet. And almost unbelievably, he did it against his will!

All of us have tools. Some people are extraordinarily gifted in wisdom. Some people are good with words. Some are exceptionally talented, and others are charismatic. How will you use what God has given you? Will you use the gifts and talents God has given you to charm others into getting your way? Or will you give your best efforts in the capacity God allows, being content with where he puts you and what he gives you to do?

For further consideration/discussion:

1. If a godly woman dates and marries a godly man, why would using her feminine guile to convince her husband to do something be against the very foundations of their relationship?

2. Some of us can be exceedingly happy that using sex appeal to our advantage isn't God's way because we wouldn't have a lot to offer. What would you say to a woman who feels passed over by opportunities and relationships because she isn't attractive in the world's eyes?

3. What tools has God (not the world) given you to express your concerns and to convince others of a better way?

Manipulating facts

Read 1 Kings 21:1-4.

Jezebel was manipulating facts long before social media made it easy. When Ahab couldn't get his way, she manipulated the situation to get him what he wanted.

You might wonder why it was such a big deal for Naboth to sell his land. Couldn't he just find another vineyard? If you've known or been a farmer with land in the family for generations, you'd understand what a big deal this was. But it was an even bigger deal than that. As Israel conquered Canaan, each tribe was given land. The tribes divided the land according to family, and the land was the family's inheritance. Families were protected from confiscation by the king; it was one power Israel's kings were not granted because keeping the inheritance was that important.[18] But that didn't keep Ahab from asking, and it certainly didn't keep him from pouting. And that's when Jezebel sprang into action. In her evil eyes, a king should get what his heart desired.

This is not too far from the mentality we easily fall into. Ask a person returning from a third world country to describe America, and "materialistic" is an obvious answer. A quick glance around our house and garage and we know it's true, but we still fall into thinking "I deserve it" and "I work hard for my money."

If we're not careful, we'll get stuck in the cycle of wanting more. Ahab had a palace. No doubt Ahab had enough. But when we let the idea of "more" grow, it's hard to be content with enough. Christians can nip this temptation in the bud by identifying it and praying about it and combating it with the Word of God.

Jezebel took a different route. She paid someone to manipulate facts in order to make it look like Naboth blasphemed God. What an interesting accusation for Jezebel to use! God's name meant nothing to her. Clearly, it meant nothing to the scoundrels she hired. It shouldn't surprise us when ungodly people with money and power manipulate facts to get what they want when it serves their purposes. They, like Jezebel, will answer to God for their actions.

God is truth, and he wants us to speak the truth. Most of us don't deliberately seek to manipulate others by distorting the facts. Sometimes it is hard to recognize when we are being manipulated. Social media sites share a common goal of wanting us to remain on their sites. They work hard to keep us there. How do they do this? They appeal to our emotions. Those videos about amazing rescues or incredible feats pull us in. But while we are scrolling, we also find information and statistics about people in positions of influence and power. Is the information we are seeing accurate? Is someone trying to manipulate our view of this world?

Documentaries have shown how social media manipulates our emotions and thought processes and works to polarize us. A classic example of this happened during the COVID-19 pandemic. Should we mask or not mask? That issue was not easy to resolve in some

---

[18] Hoerber, p. 516.

of our congregations. People had strong opinions on either side of the issue, which often reflected the arguments raging on media and social media.

How can we keep that from happening? Finding truth can be harder than it should be. Step 1 has to be to remain in God's Word. God's Word is the truth that endures through every generation, through every rumor, through every ad campaign, and through every evil government. Step 2 should be to limit the amount of time we spend not just on social media but also listening to talk shows and news shows that come with their own bias. Step 3 is to do our own investigating. Go beyond the clickbait. Search for the article. Read more than the headline to get the gist and not just the "bright lights" that pull us in. If we search for truth, we will find it, but often it will take more than a few seconds to dig deeper. Finally, we can be thankful when God sends us people to warn us and to show us what is right and true.

Maybe that sounds like too much work. It would be nice if we could just trust what was put in front of us. Unfortunately, evil doesn't take a day off. If we only believe the headlines and second- or thirdhand information, chances are good we're not getting the whole truth. When we don't know the truth, we find solace because God knows everything. He knows the truth behind the headlines, and he knows the hearts of all involved. If we don't have time to dig deep or research well, we can pray for our leaders and pray for justice to flow throughout the land. We can pray for God to be mightily involved in all areas of leadership and government. And we can rest, knowing our prayers are heard.

For further consideration/discussion:

4. Most of us are guilty of passing something along only to find out later it was not accurate or it left out an important part of the story. How can knowing that shape our social media habits?

5. What do we do when others pass information our way that is flashy and believable but not accurate?

6. When presenting our own cases, whether it is information regarding a building project at church or the best way to run an effective Sunday school, how do we use facts in such a way to convince but not mislead?

Trust and obey

Read Matthew 6:11.

Right now, you might think you are doing well because you haven't danced sexually or plotted anyone's murder to get your way. But have you ever walked all over people in the name of getting things done?

I can think of many times I was short-tempered with my children and husband while getting ready for holidays or even when I was organizing an event at church. In those moments, I didn't ask my children to help or ask my husband to do a few things. I usually reminded them of the other times they were no help at all or tried to cajole them into giving up their time for a benefit they weren't seeing. I fall into the same attitude even when the occasion is insignificant, like when I have a lot of errands to do and I'm not the nicest to those who slow me down.

For years, I saw the stained, saggy couch in our living room and suggested to my husband that we buy a new one. He wasn't bothered by its looks and would rather spend our money for a vacation or a newer car. Occasionally, I brought him furniture ads to let him know local stores were having a sale, but he brushed them aside.

I prayed, not every day but when I thought of it, for a couch. I even told God I'd like a brown leather one. A couple of years passed (yes, years!) and some friends built a new house. They called one day and asked if we were interested in their old furniture. We inherited a faux brown leather couch with recliners on both ends and a separate recliner to boot! I didn't have to go behind my husband's back or scheme to get what I wanted. I prayed, and in the Lord's good time, he provided without me having to pay a dime! That exact situation happened again a few years later with our sofa downstairs!

Jesus taught us to pray for daily bread. I'm often not content with daily bread. I want a full refrigerator with the choicest of foods. But that's not God's way. It's as if Jesus knew this would come up, because a few verses later in Matthew 6:34, he said, "Do not worry about tomorrow, for tomorrow will worry about itself. Each day has enough trouble of its own." We don't always differentiate well between need versus want. Did I need a new couch? No. The one we had, though it showed its wear, was functional.

With God's help, we can learn to be content and let go of our continual desire for more. Ask people who have moved or cleaned out a parent's house, and they will tell you the accumulation of things is not worth the effort. It's a trap we easily fall into. It's much better to treasure God and his Word and the people God has put in our lives. It's much better to be okay with a house that isn't perfect and a simple meal when people come over and to know that you have behaved in a way that respects and honors those around you.

The temptation is to strive to get what we want whatever it takes. The continual craving of our sinful nature is to get it now and not worry about anyone else. Unfortunately, our culture embraces the sinful nature's desire. We reject the idea of working to save up and waiting to get something. Credit cards make it seem everything is within our reach. Our quick, "no waiting" world leads us to think everything we want should happen now. Phrases such as "all's well that ends well" only further the idea that as long as you get the desired result, it doesn't matter how you got there.

Have you noticed how often God made his people wait? Abraham was one hundred years old when he had his first legitimate son. (When Sarah used manipulation to get a son sooner, it caused nothing but grief.) Joseph was a slave and spent years in prison before being raised to be Pharaoh's right-hand man. David too waited years after being anointed before becoming king over Judah in Hebron, and it was seven years after that when he was crowned king over all of Israel. He could have manipulated to get his way. In fact, he had the chance! But David refused to kill King Saul, even when he easily could have, and he refused to take the kingdom by force but instead waited for God to give it to him.

In the waiting, God sees our hearts. Do we trust him to provide? Do we believe he will fulfill what he promises? Do we believe he works for our good, even when we don't see the good or the good is a long way off? First Chronicles 28:9 says, "You, my son Solomon, acknowledge the God of your father, and serve him with whole-hearted devotion and with a willing mind, for the LORD searches every heart and understands every desire and every thought."

A couch, a car, or even a house is not that big of a deal in the whole scheme of things. If we're not careful, it's easy to obsess about the things that don't meet our specifications. Satan would love nothing more than for those silly little things to become obsessions and for us to dishonor our spouse, our employer, or whomever to remedy our obsession. Far better for God to remedy our hearts! When the man came to Jesus and asked him to arbitrate on his behalf concerning his inheritance, Jesus' response was to warn the man about greed.

I don't want to obsess about a couch or an outfit or what my house looks like at Christmas. If I'm going to obsess about anything, I'd rather it be that I pray continually about those coming over who have wandered from the Lord. I'd rather spend my days praying for opportunities to lead people back to the Lord. If I manipulate anything, let it be my days to be used in such a way that God is glorified in me. God sees our desires and our thoughts. May they increasingly be solely focused on serving God no matter the circumstances.

I often fail to have a trust-and-obey attitude. In sharp contrast, God has faithfully provided abundantly, even when he didn't respond to situations in the way I had hoped. He is worthy. When we are focused on God's faithfulness, then we will trust in those moments when we are waiting or feeling stuck or not in the place we want to be.

For further consideration/discussion:

7. Sometimes we don't realize how much we've taken for granted. All the years of being employed for a reliable employer vanish when workers arrive to find a note saying the company closed overnight. A cancer diagnosis makes us realize how blessed we were to have good health. What have you been taking for granted?

8. Sometimes when we finally get to the point of having what we thought we wanted, we realize we invested in and sought the wrong things. Do the things you want have an eternal component? Do you think God would want the same things for you that you want?

9. It's often easier to manipulate than to trust and obey. It's good for us to remember that while it may help us get the things we want quickly, it won't necessarily make us happy. Abraham's wife, Sarah, manipulated to have a child and suffered because of it. What blessings will be ours as a result of trusting and obeying that we can't attain through manipulation?

Key takeaways:

† The world distorts God's plan for sexuality and encourages women to use it to get what they want.

† People of the world use manipulation and trickery to get their way.

† It's good to recognize what leads us to discontent so we can avoid those things.

✝ Facts are easy to manipulate to prove a point. Sometimes we unwittingly pass along flawed information. As Christians we want to avoid this by searching out reliable news sources and being careful in what we share.

✝ God's Word is always true. Reading it will ground us in truth and keep us from getting swayed by earthly ideologies.

✝ If we trust God for daily bread, we will ask God to meet our needs instead of manipulating others to get what we want.

✝ We pray for God's will to be done. His will and ways are infinitely better than ours.

Prayer to close:

Father, keep us from manipulating others to get our way. Keep our motives pure and our hearts tuned to you. Provide us with daily bread, and help us be content. Thank you for providing far more than our daily bread. Let us use all you have given us to your glory. In Jesus our Savior we pray. Amen.

Chapter 11

The Making of
a Christian Marriage

The head and helper roles

Read 1 Corinthians 11:3 and Ephesians 5:22-24.

The ordered world we live in runs on the premise of authority. A classroom without a teacher would soon be chaotic. A fast-food restaurant without a manager would run amok. Privates listen to sergeants who listen to lieutenants who listen to captains and so on. Each fall into rank beneath the commanding officer. Managers keep everyone working toward a common goal to carry out the desires of the owner. Authority sets direction and tone.

When a Christian woman gets married, she acquires a role. Just as Christ directs, guides, and cares for the church, the man is to direct, guide, and care for his family. He is the head of the home, and his wife is his helper. This order was established at creation when God created Adam and then Eve as his helper.

The application of this concept in the home can look vastly different from house to house. Both spouses may have full-time jobs outside the home, or one or the other may have a part-time job or stay home. The division of labor can vary. If you ask 30 different families, you are likely to get 30 different answers as to how a family works. What is normal in one household would seem crazy to the next.

God entrusts the man with authority over everything and holds the man responsible for what happens in the home. That doesn't mean a wife doesn't have a say in anything or isn't allowed to make decisions. A godly man seeks and values his wife's input, listens to all the options, and determines what is best for the household. He also will make sure God's Word is taught there, grace is abundant, and forgiveness is genuine. That doesn't mean the man exclusively teaches God's Word in the home. Ideally, both husband and wife incorporate the teaching of God's Word throughout the day. But if the husband doesn't take the initiative, the wife must.

When we had two small children, I mentioned to my husband that I'd like to start having family devotions. He gave his approval, so I found a devotion book geared toward preschool children. Each night we gathered for a Bible verse, a simple story, and a prayer. Now, many years later, our nightly devotion consists of reading from the Bible followed by prayer. Though my husband isn't the one to read or pray, he leads his family in devotions each night as he gathers us together, listens intently, and makes sure the children see it as an important time.

When headship is done well, those beneath it rarely think about being in a position of submission. The head doesn't lord his position over his wife or demand his way. He works to ensure all have what they need and are following the fundamental principles the family establishes.

Sin causes tension in the head-helper relationship. Discontent festers when expectations aren't being met and when we don't feel heard. It happens when we don't value our spouse's decisions and think we can do a better job. Submission is most necessary at a point of contention. When spouses disagree, after having prayed and discussed, eventually someone needs to give. At that point, unless the husband is going against God or conscience, it is to be the wife as the helper who submits to the authority established by God.

That doesn't mean the decision is easy. It doesn't even mean it is the right decision. God sees when you submit to your husband out of obedience to him. The rest is between your husband and God. If your husband makes a bad decision, God will show him.

As a young married woman, I didn't always appreciate the roles of head and helper. I often demanded my way, refused to give in, and put my husband down. I still struggle at times. But these days I appreciate the complementary nature of our personalities and realize the value of having someone take the lead concerning what's best for our family.[19]

For further consideration/discussion:

1. Expectations cause a lot of disappointment. Think of the expectations you had going into marriage. Were they realistic? If you aren't married, what expectations do you have of your future spouse? What expectations did you have if you were married but aren't anymore?

2. A long time ago I realized I was making a fundamental mistake. When I wasn't getting along with my husband, I saw him as the enemy. Eventually, I realized Satan was the enemy. God and my husband were my allies. How does this change the way you handle disagreements?

3. How does the concept of head and helper go against worldly standards and ideals for women?

---

[19] For more on the head-helper principle, study *Heirs Together* by Richard Gurgel and Kathie Wendland. Student materials and a leader's guide are available for purchase online at nph.net or by calling 800-662-6022.

Submitting made easier

Read Matthew 20:25-28; 1 Corinthians 7:2-6; and Ephesians 5:33.

Satan is only too happy to cause dissonance in marriage. Once frustration occurs, it easily leads to disagreements, arguments, and hurt feelings. God has given us weapons to use to fortify our marriage so that it stands up against Satan, our sinful nature, and the false ideology of the world. Making spiritual growth a priority makes submitting to our husband easier. As we grow spiritually, we grow in godliness and desire to do things God's way.

Jesus taught his disciples that worldly leadership is considerably different than leadership in his kingdom. While worldly leaders strive for prominence and to be served by others, godly leaders look for opportunities to serve. Godly leadership is caring, helping, and working together, not demanding that others serve you. Jesus gave his disciples a wonderful example of servant leadership when he washed his disciples' feet. The apostle John tells us:

> When he had finished washing their feet, he put on his clothes and returned to his place. "Do you understand what I have done for you?" he asked them. "You call me 'Teacher' and 'Lord,' and rightly so, for that is what I am. Now that I, your Lord and Teacher, have washed your feet, you also should wash one another's feet. I have set you an example that you should do as I have done for you." (John 13:12-15)

We don't stay spiritually strong without feeding on God's Word. Isaiah 55:10,11 says, "As the rain and the snow come down from heaven, and do not return to it without watering the earth and making it bud and flourish, so that it yields seed for the sower and bread for the eater, so is my word that goes out from my mouth: It will not return to me empty, but will accomplish what I desire and achieve the purpose for which I sent it." The Holy Spirit works through the Word to convict and sharpen, bestow wisdom, and encourage. Being in the Word draws us into a closer relationship with God. The Word also softens our hard hearts and helps us to be more gracious and ready to forgive. Experiencing and understanding God's grace through Bible study motivates us to leave our selfishness and embrace selflessness as we aim to give the same comfort we have been given.

Blessings abound as we take advantage of opportunities to grow spiritually and encourage our husbands to do the same. Submitting to a godly husband is not a burden but a pleasure. And that is why Satan will do everything he can to keep you from the Word. *Join that group Bible study? No way do you have time for that! An in-home Bible study with people you don't know? Sounds awful, uncomfortable, and intrusive! Who has time for Sunday morning Bible study? After all, Sunday is family day, and doesn't God want family to spend time together?*

Take it from someone who knows Satan's lies all too well. Confront Satan's lies, get into the Word every opportunity you can, and your marriage will benefit exponentially. Being around other Christian wives and couples and being encouraged in the Word always lead to blessings.

The apostle Paul reminds us of another weapon we have at our disposal. He tells the husband to give his body to his wife and the wife to give her body to her husband (mutual submission). In fact, the only reason Paul suggests we deny each other sexually is to spend time in prayer and that only by mutual consent. God designed sexual intimacy to be the glue that bonds spouses together. When husband and wife make sexual intimacy a priority, both are more likely to be kind, loving, and generous to the other.

It's easy to put intimacy on the back burner. Rarely does it become a priority without intentionality. Our habits can easily become a stumbling block. One spouse may watch TV late into the night; the other fails to put down the phone. Overeating and overdrinking can affect your libido too. Ignoring each other sexually can be one more part of a vicious cycle of discord and conflict.

The third thing that is key in our relationship to our husbands might sound trite, but it's monumental. Women need love. Men need respect. God told men to love their wives and reminded women to respect their husbands. Practically speaking, it comes down to word choice, tone of voice, making your husband a priority, and taking his ideas seriously. If you're not careful, you can run yourself ragged running after your children while ignoring your husband's simple requests.

More often than not, I was conflicted on Sunday mornings. My husband wanted to leave just a few minutes after the church service ended. I have many friends I see only at church, and I was involved in various church activities. It was par for the course for someone or several people to stop me to chat about one of those activities. I didn't want to ignore those people, but having my husband wait in the vehicle with the kids seemed disrespectful. The solution was as simple as me driving separately to church. We don't live far from church, so it was a small thing that made everyone happy. My husband could go home right away with the children who wanted to go, and those who wanted to stay behind and chat for a while were able to do that too.

Often, being respectful is a matter of small choices. It's choosing silence when it would be easy to complain. It is overlooking something he does instead of putting him down. It's appreciating what he does well instead of focusing on what he does poorly.

For further consideration/discussion:

4. The pastor who married us told us he put having sex with his wife on his calendar to make sure it happened. At first, that might sound silly. In truth, it's pretty smart. Like anything else, intimacy can easily fall by the wayside unless we are deliberate. What obstacles get in the way of intimacy? What can you do to overcome those obstacles?

5. Just like intimacy, spiritual growth is best when it's deliberate. What are you going to do to grow spiritually? What can you do to encourage spiritual growth with your spouse? Who can you enlist to help?

6. When are you most likely to be disrespectful? My husband tends to talk while we're watching TV. Instead of pausing the program, asking a question, chatting, and resuming the program, he blurts out his comments, which means I miss whatever is happening on the screen. I tend to get snippy when he does this. These days when he starts to talk, I push pause or ask him to do so, so we can discuss without me being irritated. What is your action plan to keep disrespect out of your conversations?

Submitting to an unbeliever

Read 1 Peter 3:1,2.

Many Christian women find themselves in this predicament. Maybe their husbands weren't Christians when they married, or maybe faith wasn't important at that time. But then, by God's grace, God used something to reawaken faith. What hope does a woman have if her husband is not a Christian or if her husband doesn't value her faith or lead well?

Jesus submitted for the greater good of providing redemption for humankind. If submitting is a means of bringing someone to Christ, what a worthy endeavor! That is what the apostle Peter asks us to keep in mind. Treating your husband with kindness and being attentive to his needs might soften his heart to the Holy Spirit's promptings. Even if it doesn't, it's going to make for a more peaceful home.

But that doesn't mean it is easy. Prayer is vital in this undertaking, prayer that persists even when we don't see change. Long ago I heard about a woman who prayed for years that her husband would come to faith and go to church. He came to church for her funeral and every week after until the Lord took him home. She didn't live to see her prayers answered, but they were answered just the same.

Prayers are not just for your husband's change of heart but also for strength to love him well. As the apostle Paul said in 2 Corinthians 4:17,18, "Our light and momentary troubles are achieving for us an eternal glory that far outweighs them all. So we fix our eyes not on what is seen, but on what is unseen, since what is seen is temporary, but what is unseen is eternal."

Everyday circumstances could bog us down. Rarely are we able to see change happen in front of us. But that doesn't mean God isn't using our example and our kind words and faithful encouragement to work in our husbands' hearts. Rather than worry about the day-to-day and lament when we don't see growth or change, we can set our hearts on eternity. Pray simple prayers throughout your day. *Use me to show him you, Lord. Bring him to saving faith. Soften his heart. Thwart Satan's attempts to keep him from coming to faith.*

God is in charge of the time frame and the method. Jesus didn't force anyone to follow him. But when people did follow him, it was love, not nagging, that served as the conduit to change. The apostle Paul reminds us that love is patient and kind, not rude. It protects, hopes, and perseveres. Love is the action plan (1 Corinthians 13).

Don't hesitate to ask others to pray for you. A godly woman who will pray for you and encourage you when weariness settles in can be a lifesaver. It is hard to carry a heavy load, but it's so much easier when you have another to share the weight.

And don't forget the friend who is with you 24/7. The apostle Paul told Timothy when everyone else deserted him: "The Lord stood at my side and gave me strength" (2 Timothy 4:17). God is that friend who will never leave you, who will listen to you at 3 o'clock in the morning or 11 o'clock at night. God will collect your tears and give you the strength to keep going.

For further consideration/discussion:

7. Maybe you married a Christian man who over time has been pulled into worldly ways and away from God. What might you do to change direction after years of going the wrong way?

8. Often we are too embarrassed to mention our husband's spiritual condition to our Christian friends. Why might we bring it up, and how can we do so in such a way that we respect and honor him?

9. Rarely does a problem go away on its own. High blood pressure left unattended gets worse, not better, and causes more damage. A cavity not filled grows. And yet too often—day after day, week after week, month after month—we let our spiritual condition slide. Why is today the day to make a plan and change that?

Key takeaways:

+ God designed the man to be the head of the home and the woman to be the helper in marriage.

+ Spiritual maturity will help us serve one another in love.

+ Making sex a priority in marriage serves to bond the relationship and makes it easier to serve each other.

+ Men crave respect the way women crave love. Choosing a respectful tone and words will likely lead to a more favorable response from your spouse.

+ Our thoughtful and kind actions as a godly spouse will prayerfully lead our husbands to give thanks to God. At the very least, it will make for a more peaceful home for ourselves and our children.

Prayer to close:

Heavenly Father, thank you for showing abundant love to us. Forgive us for the times we've failed to listen to you. Remind us that your way is best. Help us submit willingly and bless our marriages. In Jesus' powerful name we pray. Amen.

CHAPTER 12
A Gentle and Quiet Spirit Submits

God's plan for the church

Read 1 Timothy 2:11-15 and Titus 2:3-5.

It's important to read the Bible in its context as a whole. It can be dangerous to pick one or two passages to stand on their own (as I did above). It is equally dangerous to disregard a passage of Scripture saying it is no longer relevant. Scripture does not contradict itself or have an expiration date. Serious study reveals the wisdom that is easily missed if we quickly brush over passages we don't understand. Satan uses our misunderstandings of Scripture to keep us from digging deeper or asking questions of those who lead.

In 1 Timothy, Paul does not prohibit women from teaching. We know this to be true, because in his letter to Titus, Paul tells the older women to teach the younger women. Paul is reminding the church of the authority God established in the creation of head and helper. (If you haven't studied the Bible study *Heirs Together*, I recommend it as fundamental to understanding this premise.)

This is not to say there aren't times for a woman to teach men in the church. Sometimes men specifically call on a woman to speak to them about a certain topic. Our parish nurse often addresses the church regarding how we as a congregation can stay physically healthy. Sometimes women are called to attend a meeting to offer expertise in a certain area. I served on a committee to determine which ministries in our church were working well and which should be altered to better fit our mission. After a ten-month study, we were called before the church council and elders to report our findings. We weren't teaching Scripture with authority, and we, a group of men and women, were there by invitation.

Scripture also gives examples of men and women ministering within their homes. Priscilla and Aquila were a husband-and-wife team that ministered to Apollos. After hearing him speak at the synagogue, they invited Apollos to their home "and explained to him the way of God more adequately" (Acts 18:26). Later, the church met in their home. Priscilla is always mentioned with Aquila. Clearly, God gifted Priscilla with the ability to explain and apply God's Word, which she did in conjunction with her husband.

Another example is found in Acts 21:8,9: "Leaving the next day, we reached Caesarea and stayed at the house of Philip the evangelist, one of the Seven. He had four unmarried daughters who prophesied." As with Priscilla, these daughters seemed to be doing ministry, primarily in the home, alongside a man, in this case their father.

In Judges chapter 4, Deborah gave Barak a message from the Lord. He was to go with ten thousand men to the top of Mount Tabor. God would lead the enemies of Israel there and give them into Barak's hands. Though Deborah gave simple instructions and the assurance of victory, Barak was still timid and asked Deborah to go with him. She agreed and willingly climbed the mountain to support him. Then, when the time of battle came, she encouraged Barak, reminding him that God was with him.

When our brothers in Christ are timid about leading a Bible study, women, especially those gifted in teaching, can come alongside our brothers and encourage them. We can walk with them, encouraging them to lead and giving them tools to do so. We can pray for them and build them up. Instead of pushing them out of the way, we can walk alongside our brothers and participate in the study in such a way to direct the conversation when they struggle.

For further consideration/discussion:

1. Teaching doesn't happen just in a group setting. Mentoring can happen between two people. Take a close look at your church and/or your Christian school. Whose lives can you impact by taking them under your wing and nurturing them in the Lord?

2. Think of two or three men in the congregation you could build up to do God's work. How could you come alongside them and support them while being cognizant of boundaries that will protect your marriage and theirs?

3. Have there been times you've felt slighted at church because you are a woman? How do we address those issues in a godly way?

Submission to authority

Read Romans 13:1-7.

Like it or not, we are all under authority. When we are at odds with leadership, the temptation is to complain, insult those over us, and blame them for the problem. That's not God's way. The apostle Paul makes it clear: God establishes authority without our consent. If our pick for president, senator, or city council doesn't win, God still expects us to respect the winner. If the manager we love leaves to take a different position and the new manager is clumsy or clueless, God still expects us to respect, obey, and give our best effort to the new manager.

How my sinful nature longs for terms and conditions of my own making! "Submit to the leaders you agree with!" or "Obey those who earn your respect!" Then I could justifiably scoff at the incompetent ones and only give my efforts to those I deem qualified. I would happily wash my hands of paying undue respect to anyone who doesn't share my convictions. That is, after all, what the unbelieving world does. But God calls his children to live with absolute trust, not in our earthly leaders but in God who is ultimately in control.

God gave us plenty of examples in his Word of those who did this well. Joseph served Potiphar, the jailer, and a heathen pharaoh. He worked hard and gave his best efforts and was elevated to leadership as a result. Daniel, Shadrach, Meshach, and Abednego served Nebuchadnezzar, a ruthless king who, despite seeing God work mightily time after time, continued in his pagan beliefs. Esther served Xerxes, even though his arrogance took young women from their homes to serve his sexual whims, and even though he was rash enough to agree to the annihilation of an entire race.

But perhaps the best example is David, who refused to kill Saul even though David had been anointed and Saul was not a good king. David could have used many circumstances as justification to rebel against or even kill Saul.

- When Saul returned from a battle where he failed to complete the mission God gave him, the first thing on his agenda was to set up a monument in his honor. He didn't even realize God wasn't pleased with his half-hearted obedience (1 Samuel 15).

- Saul didn't step up to fight Goliath even though he was taller and older than David. His troops shook with fear, and Saul did nothing to encourage them in the Lord (1 Samuel 17).

- Saul was sitting under a tree when his son Jonathan went to the Philistine outpost and took charge of the situation (1 Samuel 14).

- Instead of governing, Saul spent time and resources chasing David in an effort to secure the throne for his family (1 Samuel 23). Despite these failures, David refused to harm him and refused to rejoice when he learned of his death.

We too are to distinguish ourselves by our obedience and submission and our refusal to speak ill of those God puts over us. That doesn't mean we have to remain quiet when those in authority do wrong. We should exercise our freedom of speech to denounce injustice. If we're being asked to do something against God's Word and our conscience (even something secular society deems as okay and, in some cases, even loving), we should make every effort to voice our concern and even exercise the freedom we have to refuse. Mordecai told Esther of the plot to kill the Jews. He urged her to speak up because she was in a position to have an audience with the king. The ten Boom family members recognized their status as Christians and used their privilege to rescue Jews from Nazi prejudice and extermination—at great cost to their family. Neither Mordecai nor the ten Booms resorted to flagrant denunciation. To do so likely would have resulted in death. Instead, they did what they could: prayed and put their faith in God who was bigger than the most powerful authority of the time.

For further consideration/discussion:

4. Read Hebrews 13:17. What is our duty at work, home, church, or government when it comes to those who are over us?

5. Why is it to our benefit when our leaders find joy in their work?

6. Name some ways that disrespecting those in authority is commonplace. What will you do to stand apart and be different?

Submitting like Jesus

Read Luke 2:51.

Submission carries the connotation of being beneath another or less than. And, oh, how the concept has been abused, even under the guise of Christianity! But that perversion shouldn't deter us from understanding what is at the heart of submission. While submission isn't politically correct and is categorically despised by many women, we can take comfort in the example given to us in Jesus, who was obedient to his Father and submitted to his will.

Jesus was obedient to Mary and Joseph. Jesus, sovereign over everything and Creator of the universe, left heaven to be raised by his sinful parents. Take a minute to imagine Jesus' life as a child. Imagine Mary teaching Jesus about God. Imagine Jesus' siblings and the arguments that must have taken place. When the siblings plotted mischief, Jesus refused to partake. Was he ridiculed? What were the conversations between Jesus and his siblings? Was he persecuted for being perfect, a teacher's pet, mama's boy, etc.?

Jesus continually exhibited restraint. He submitted to his Father's will, which was proclaimed already in Genesis 3:15: "I will put enmity between you and the woman, and between your offspring and hers; he will crush your head, and you will strike his heal."

The Godhead—Father, Son, and Holy Spirit—operated in complete unity. They weren't flipping coins to see who would go to earth to suffer and die. How do we know? By examining Jesus' life. The apostle John made sure we understood Jesus' submission. In the account of the woman at the well, we read this statement: "Now [Jesus] had to go through Samaria" (John 4:4). If we were to look at a map of the Holy Land, we would see Jesus started near the Jordan River in Judea. Galilee was in the north and Samaria was between. We would think nothing of that verse and the idea that Jesus had to go through Samaria. The footnote in my study Bible says, "The necessity lay in Jesus' mission, not in geography."[20] The People's Bible explains further. Jesus didn't have to go through Samaria because it was the only route from Judea to Galilee. In fact, there

---

[20] Hoerber, p. 1,609.

were three routes, and the other two, the one to the east and the other to the west, were preferential to Jews who wanted to stay out of Samaria. Jesus *had* to go through Samaria because he had a divine appointment with an outcast who would be instrumental in bringing her whole town to faith.[21] Jesus planned his route and his day in accordance with his Father's will.

John 5:19 records Jesus talking about his Father: "The Son can do nothing by himself; he can do only what he sees his Father doing, because whatever the Father does the Son also does." That is a submission most of us will never know. Often I fail to submit in my marriage, employment, and country. I struggle because of my sinful nature.

Jesus' attitude was different. The apostle Paul wrote in Philippians 2:6-8, "[Jesus], who, being in very nature God, did not consider equality with God something to be used to his own advantage; rather, he made himself nothing by taking the very nature of a servant, being made in human likeness. And being found in appearance as a man, he humbled himself by becoming obedient to death—even death on a cross!"

To put this in perspective, even though Jesus was true God and qualified to run the show, he put aside his right to do so and submitted both to heavenly and human authority for the sake of a greater good, namely, our salvation.

My sinful nature doesn't want to submit and certainly not on the occasions when I think I know best. Too often I've demanded my way only to realize my way wasn't best. I know that Jesus forgives me, and I need the Spirit's help to become more like Jesus.

For further consideration/discussion:
   7. Most of us have people we happily submit to. There are others
      who are far more difficult to submit to. Who do you, or would
      you, struggle to submit to?

---

[21] Gary Baumler, *John*, of The People's Bible series (Milwaukee: Northwestern Publishing House, 1997) pp. 60,61.

8. Jesus yielded to the will of his Father and others whole-heartedly, with complete sincerity and commitment. If I'm honest I submit often enough but not always wholeheartedly and not always with the same objective as Jesus. What is the difference between submitting for the sake of submitting and submitting wholeheartedly?

9. What does Jesus' example teach us about submitting to those less qualified, less tactful, or less knowledgeable?

Key takeaways:

+ God established the authority of the church. He, in infinite wisdom, called men to pastor and lead the church.

+ The New Testament shows women as active members in the ministry of the church.

+ Our job is to use our gifts and talents within the confines of God's commands. In doing so, God is glorified, and we are valuable members of God's church on earth.

+ Godly men and women will recognize God as the true authority and submit to those he's placed over us, even when we don't agree with their actions or beliefs.

+ God's Word gives us many examples of people working under heathen rulers and doing so with respect and an excellent work ethic.

+ God's Word reminds us that it is in our best interest to work for the greater good and to make our leaders' lives a joy, not a burden. When we can't in good conscience follow a law, we ought to respectfully attempt to be exempt from it, and in doing so, shine a light on God's Word and ways.

✝ Jesus submitted to Mary and Joseph while living in their house. If Jesus, true God from eternity, who created the world, was willing to submit to flawed humans, we should be willing to do the same.

✝ Jesus was able to keep his perspective. He submitted for a greater good. We need to remember our submission is also for a greater good (peace in the home, the church, the community, or the workplace).

Prayer to close:

Jesus, thank you for your quiet submission and your willingness to submit to flawed mortals. Teach me to be more like you. Motivate me with the enormous love that motivated you. When worldly leaders do things that pain you and are against your Word, remind me to be bold in proclaiming the truth and help me stand firm in your ways. Help me remember that this world will never be perfect, but in time you will bring me to your kingdom to live in perfect righteousness. Jesus, in your name I pray. Amen.

Conclusion

When my name comes into a conversation, I can guess, with 100 percent probability, that the words *gentle and quiet* have never come up.

Spirited, likely.

Bold, maybe.

Crazy, almost certainly.

Remember, though, that it is a gentle and quiet *spirit* that is of great worth in God's sight. *Spirit* may be defined as the character, attitude, and thoughts that shape a person. A gentle spirit knows God is in control in the middle of the storm. I can be bold to say so and to reassure others that this is true. *Bold* is not synonymous with *harsh*, as long as I'm not condescending or arrogant.

When my family hits a snag, I'm not sitting in the corner waiting for someone else to figure out what's going on. I may have no idea how we're getting out of this mess, but I'm one million percent sure of God's faithfulness and that he hears when we call. And I'll be quick to remind my family.

It's not a problem to see or recognize a leader not leading well. The problem is in choosing to overtake instead of walking alongside or to gossip about instead of confronting in a biblical way.

There is so much to having a gentle and quiet spirit. These studies challenge me, but not in a give-up-because-you'll-never-get-it way. They challenge me the way God's law always challenges. It shows a better way and the path of blessing. I'll never get it right all the time. But that's not the point.

Jesus already did.

When we put these lessons into practice, we reap the blessings, even if things don't change. Obedience when it's hard proves we trust God. We'll keep doing it the way he wants even if change never happens.

As wives and mothers and sisters and daughters, we have plenty of battles to fight and kingdom work to do. When our work is done with a gentle and quiet spirit, then God's will has been done in our lives.

That's what I want. And I'm guessing that's what you want too.

Answer Guide

Chapter 1

1. Answers will vary.

2. Answers will vary.

3. Answers will vary.

4. Time always comes up as an answer. It is important to realize that we make time for things that are important to us. Satan works to keep us from the Word because he knows when we get in the Word, we'll grow closer to God.

5. If Jesus in his humanity needed to pray, how much more do we?! God will arm us for every battle as we come to him in prayer.

6. Jesus got up while it was still dark. He gave up time he could be sleeping to go meet with his Father in prayer. He also went to an isolated place. It's not always easy to find a place completely free of distraction. When my children were young, sometimes I read the Bible while sitting on the couch, with them playing on the floor in front of me. But my main Bible reading time was in the evening after everyone was in bed. One time and place doesn't fit everyone. The important thing is that we find time to spend with God—reading the Bible and in prayer.

7. Psalm 119:28—The Word will strengthen us. As we read examples of God rescuing his people and as we see his faithfulness, our faith will be strengthened and we'll be reminded to trust.

   Psalm 119:36,37—The Word turns our hearts from things of the world to eternal things.

   Psalm 119:49,50—Scripture shows us that God sees us in our struggles. He may not remove us from struggles immediately. Joseph was in prison for two years; David was on the run from Saul for many years—but God provided for both during the struggle. Scripture gives us hope and reminds us of God's promises.

   Psalm 119:104—The Word gives us discernment and understanding so we don't get sucked into the wrong things. It guides our path.

   Psalm 119:160—God's Word is true! We can't always believe much of what we read or hear, but God's Word is always true!

   Psalm 119:165—God's Word offers us peace from the frenzied world! We have peace in God's promises and peace knowing God has our lives in his view.

8. Luke 9:62—If you didn't watch where you were going, you might not plow a straight row. Jesus was saying we shouldn't be constantly looking at all the things we could be doing if we weren't doing ministry. He's after wholehearted devotion.

   Luke 17:7-10—Our service should be done humbly, knowing God has done much for us and we are not worthy of him.

   Romans 12:11—When we realize all that God's done for us, it's easy to serve him zealously and wholeheartedly.

9. We're forgetting how many people would love to help but can't or aren't in situations that allow them to help. Those of us who have been given much, as Jesus said in Luke 12:48, should rejoice that we are able to serve God!

10. Remember Mary! We all need to take time for the Word. That is where we find our rest. And remember Jesus! He wasn't overwhelmed by the crowds. He did what he determined to do and moved on. We can only do what we can do. Sometimes we need to learn to ask for help at home or in our ministry.

Chapter 2

1. We probably aren't able to see the effect this storm will have on our lives. It may look messy now, but that doesn't mean it won't be beautiful eventually. All projects are messy when they're in progress, but we keep going, knowing the end result is worth it.

2. God is not sadistic. Something good will come of our storm. We can wait out the storm while praying that we learn God's will and bring God glory in and through the chaos.

3. Walk with them. Listen. Check in often. Send a comforting text or Bible verse.

4. Demands imply we deserve something, or we aren't getting our due.

5. We often waste time telling and retelling our complaints to anyone who will listen. Instead of wasting time talking with people who may not have any means of helping us, we can go straight to God. He sees the whole situation and has the power to remedy it.

6. In doing so, we are insulting the very One capable of helping us. Scripture assures us that God hears our prayers and is not blind to our situation. It is far better to go to God humbly and reverently for help.

7. We need all the promises God gives us in his Word. As you read his Word, underline or circle words of comfort. Take note of how God took care of his people in the past. We can take Jesus' words to heart, including all things are possible with God (Matthew 19:26); you are worth more than many

sparrows (Matthew 10:31); and do not worry about tomorrow (Matthew 6:34).

8. We sometimes accuse God of putting us in predicaments, even predicaments that are consequences of our sin! We overspend and accuse God of not providing. We fail to make our health a priority and accuse God of allowing us to be sick. Naomi assumed God's hand was against her. We don't know the circumstances of her husband's or sons' deaths, but we can be sure God wasn't out to get Naomi. Though she accused him of making her life bitter, the entire book of Ruth shows God's mercy and providence.

9. In the middle of the storm, I need the help of the Holy Spirit to say and do as I ought. He can put a right spirit in me to do so. I'm asking him to remind me of my salvation and all the joy that brings. I have heaven ahead of me. The troubles here are momentary in the whole scheme of things. Ultimately, I'm asking him to hold me and walk me through the storm.

Chapter 3

1. I would love to say I always turn to God first, but I have too often complained, fretted, worried, and gone through a mental barrage of worst-case scenarios instead of turning to God first.

2. Answers will vary.

3. Pray. Prayer should always be our first resort. Jesus told us not to worry, because we are loved by our heavenly Father. We have to quit looking at the circumstances and start looking at our Savior.

4. Often we selectively remember the good memories without remembering the struggles of the past, just as the Israelites longed for the food without remembering the hard lives of being slaves. It's easy to fall into discontent. It's far better for us to find blessings in every situation.

5. Deuteronomy 31:6—God is with us, and he's strong enough for any storm.

Isaiah 49:16—God hasn't forgotten us. Our issues are always before him.

Romans 8:38,39—The issues that might separate us from loved ones and friends (leaving a job, moving into a nursing home, or any number of issues) will not separate us from God. He's with us 24/7/365.

6. Answers will vary.

7. When Asaph couldn't see the good, he chose to meditate on God's past miracles. God had been faithful in the past. He doesn't change, so surely he is still faithful, even when we don't see it clearly now.

8. We can record in a journal the ways God has worked, or we can talk about them often in order to keep them in mind. Some people write down how God worked; they put those pieces of paper in a jar to be read at the end of the year. I have many Scripture wall hangings in my house as constant reminders to look to God for deliverance. It doesn't matter what it is—a wall hanging, a piece of jewelry, a shirt, or a song we play over and over—we, like the Israelites, need physical reminders that God is faithful.

9. Our testimony and the way God carried us can encourage others. That's not to say we should broadcast every situation we've been in. But as we see opportunity, we can share the way God worked in and through our difficult situations.

Chapter 4

1. Answers will vary.

2. Answers will vary.

3. Answers will vary.

4. We do this when we plant seeds of discontent. We mention how much the pastor bugs us or how annoying the organist is. We do this when we complain about the songs and the way things are done instead of being joyful about our house of worship and those who serve there. We do it outside of the church by saying we wouldn't put up with the behavior of a spouse or child.

5. We can stir up trouble with a phone call, text message, e-mail, or post on social media.

6. It's easier to say things from behind a screen than to say them to someone's face. In person we'd likely be more tactful, and we'd be able to see the person's reaction.

7. We know seasons of struggle can lead to great spiritual renewal and growth. It's easy to complain. Far better to remind our friends of God's faithfulness and anticipate how God might work through and in our situations.

8. Answers will vary.

9. A spiritually mature Christian friend can be a blessing to help us do this. And it's always good to pray and ask God for wisdom and insight into the situation.

10. The Word will redirect our thoughts. The Holy Spirit will renew our minds. Focusing on truth rather than emotions will give us a better view of what is going on. Recognizing Satan's tactics will keep us from falling for them. The gospel reminds us of God's forgiveness when we've fallen short.

Chapter 5

1. Some gossip magazines pay people for inside information, so money could be a motive. Revenge might fuel someone who has been hurt to spread lies or information about another. Jealousy could be another factor. It could be a desire for attention, to be liked or to get on someone else's good side.

2. These things take time. We shouldn't be quick to judge but should wait for the information to be sorted out. In the meantime, we can pray for truth and patiently wait to know more if it's important for us.

3. When an egregious rumor comes out, it may be a good idea to discuss the situation with your family. Sometimes it's beneficial for teaching how to avoid the same situation. Often "big" rumors are brought up in the confines of a Bible study. That too is a good place to discuss how Satan works, traps, and pulls us in. It's also a great time to pray for all involved.

4. This is such an important distinction! We all need to be able to "bleed"—to pour out our souls—to someone. It is not sinful to go to someone when you have concerns about another person whose actions are impacting you. A godly friend can bring clarity to an otherwise confusing situation. They can encourage you, pray for you, and even, like Jonathan, serve as a go-between, possibly bringing about peace.

5. Our job is not to set the record straight, especially if it means telling confidential information. Our job is to leave it to God and let him set the record straight.

6. Fortification always comes from time spent in the Word. As we daily go to the Word, we are built up. That doesn't mean things won't shock us or take us off guard, but God's Word will prepare us, and the Spirit will sustain us.

7. We will live very differently than the world. If that's the case, they may see us as odd and mock us.

8. God knows the truth. We all fall short, but God's grace covers all of it. His children should always surround the people caught in rumors (instead of running away from them) and lovingly, with law and gospel, guide them to peace. This too will pass.

9. If it's a minor subject, you may choose to overlook it. If not, go to the person humbly. Say that you heard something and

you don't know if it's true, but it's important to you that this friend knows the truth.

Chapter 6

1. Answers will vary, but often we overlook that others are not the enemy. Satan is causing division. We often fail to put the best construction on others' words and actions.

2. On any given day I need to work on all of them! I don't want to be quarrelsome and resentful. I want to be gentle in word choice and tone. I want my words to instruct, not alienate. I want my deepest desire to be their repentance, not my being right.

3. My sinful nature. I so often fail to make it the priority it should be and rely on my own devices instead of God.

4. Mostly pride. If I think I'm right, too often I charge ahead without worrying about hurting the other person. Sometimes I'm impatient and expect spiritual maturity from people who are still young in their faith.

5. We had spent time in the Word, worshiped, and prayed. Doing so softens a heart. The Holy Spirit was at work to open my heart before my friend ever said a word.

6. Jesus taught the truth and let the truth pierce hearts. He continually brought an eternal perspective. He didn't get sidetracked with details that didn't matter but kept to the heart of the issue.

7. Unfortunately, yes and yes. To do so is to deny God's omniscience. In truth, he knows the situation better than we do. He knows motives and thoughts and intentions. It's far better for us to humbly ask God to intervene, knowing he knows everything and can do what's best for all involved.

8. Answers will vary.

9. It's good to test the waters: to offer a little advice and see how people respond. It can also be useful to ask if people want your advice. If they don't or if they seem defensive, it's best to keep it to yourself and keep them in prayer.

Chapter 7

1. Answers will vary, but some common answers may be other people's nicely decorated homes; their spouses who might seem so much better than yours; or their seemingly accomplished children; and the like.

2. When we become consumed with other people's lives, we aren't thoroughly invested in our own. Far better to pour ourselves into our family, career, or church than to longingly look at someone else's. The family suffers when we bring unnecessary drama into the family. It is good to help others, but sometimes it is best when we let others work it out themselves.

3. It's a blessing to have a friend who says something like "Is this something you can change?" or "Is this worth the emotional toll it seems to be taking from you?"

4. I've found it's best to stay on topic. When I ask a question and the answer becomes "She or he always . . ." I try to redirect by saying something like "Let's work on this issue." Martin Luther encouraged us in the Eighth Commandment to take our neighbor's thoughts, words, and actions in the kindest possible way. When we think well of them (*They didn't mean to hurt me*, or *They must have forgotten*), we allow God to be God. If their intentions are different, he'll deal with it.

5. For me, it's when I'm tired.

6. I need to turn off the phone and take a nap or go to bed. Also, when I remember that scrolling changes nothing, I'm more likely to turn to prayer.

7. Praying, reading the Bible, and connecting with a spiritually mature friend are good places to start.

8. It's good to remember to be discerning about what we post. Posts made during emotional times could backfire. Far better to deal with the situation out of the public eye.

9. Answers will vary.

10. Answers will vary.

11. Answers will vary.

Chapter 8

1. When I know God is bigger than my problems, I go to him and ask for wisdom, direction, and intervention. When I am driven by fear, I am more likely to complain to God like the disciples and the Israelites did.

2. We fortify our faith in the Word: "Faith comes from hearing the message, and the message is heard through the word about Christ" (Romans 10:17). It is important to make Bible reading a regular part of our day, not just when we need help but always. Faith will remind us of God's power and all the times he's rescued his people in the past.

3. Our complaints are an insult to God. We aren't trusting him as a loving Father, and we aren't trusting him as an all-powerful God.

4. Our complaints may be saying, "God, how dare you allow me to have hardship?" A better prayer is "Lord, how can I glorify you even in this situation?"

5. Answers will vary. When we have a servant's heart, we wait on the Lord. We take what he gives us and thank him whatever the situation. When we maintain our composure and trust God to work things out, we testify to others that God is worthy of our allegiance and trust.

6. The sassy child who comes from a broken home needs our love, not our condemnation. Every broken person needs Jesus. Every time we offer love to anyone, we are the hands and feet

of Christ. Jesus asks us to see him in the face of whomever we help. I would never turn away from Jesus. Therefore I should always be ready to help whomever he sends my way.

7. Perhaps frustration, exhaustion, and being overwhelmed, among others.

8. They never... Why do I always get...? How come things never work out for me?

9. It starts by recognizing that complaining is a useless endeavor that offends God. All true change begins in the heart. In the world we're bombarded with ideologies that applaud being selfish and looking out for our own interests. Getting into the Word will realign us with the truth of God. Our faith will be strengthened, and we will see the benefit of trusting rather than complaining.

Chapter 9

1. Jesus told the people to be on their guard against greed.

2. Probably the biggest blessing is to have a dependence on God. When we find security in anything other than God, our hope is on something that can change in an instant. It's also good to have goals and to work toward those goals. Persistence makes us stronger. Working together as a family or church family toward a common goal solidifies relationships.

3. Ideally, I would always treasure souls first and foremost and keep the things of God in first place in my life. To make service in God's kingdom a priority, I may need to shift some things around. That may look different in each of our lives.

4. Answers will vary.

5. I don't want to take service away from someone else. There's no reason for me to struggle in an area I am not gifted to serve while people who are gifted in that area aren't using

their gifts. Trying to serve where I'm not gifted to serve leads to frustration.

6. Answers will vary.

7. Answers will vary.

8. Answers will vary. Either extreme could hinder your salvation. The prideful person doesn't believe she needs God's help, and the person who thinks her sin is too big for God to forgive doesn't acknowledge Jesus' sacrifice as adequate.

9. Answers will vary.

Chapter 10

1. A godly woman recognizes and appreciates the role the husband has as head of the household. Rather than undermine his authority, she'll work beside and with him, encouraging him.

2. Walk with the Lord. Be faithful to God and his Word. He will do a far better job of taking care of you. The world loves people as long as they look the way the world wants them to look. When youth fades or fads change, the world tosses people aside to idolize the next thing.

3. Christian women abound with godly wisdom and sanctified common sense. Together with love and patience, these make every Christian woman a powerful influencer. Christian women look to God's Word and the Spirit's guidance in applying it. Finally, do not underestimate the power of your prayers.

4. I rarely post or share anything publicly apart from Bible verses or quotes. I know the Bible is true.

5. First, don't pass it on. Then, if you think or know it's inaccurate and it's posted publicly on your social media wall, remove it from your page. In my experience, it's rarely worth the energy to do anything more. Confronting someone about an online incident has not gone well for me in the past, so I don't waste the energy trying anymore.

6. Present the facts and listen humbly, being open to ideas from others. I learned a long time ago that my ideas are not always the best and having other people's input is a blessing.

7. Answers will vary.

8. Answers will vary.

9. We will know we submitted to our heavenly Father and his will for our lives. We can have peace and contentment knowing God loves us, gives us good gifts, and works for our good.

Chapter 11

1. My expectations were not realistic. I didn't foresee disagreements. I thought we would agree on most things. I didn't understand the concept of a head-helper relationship or how vital it was to make prayer and Bible reading a part of our relationship.

2. Now I pray first and often. I pray proactively that we get on the same page and stay on the same page about the direction we want to go. I know it's okay to take a break from talking about something we disagree on, think on it, pray on it, and come back to it.

3. The world tells women to fight for power and to demand their ways. The world certainly doesn't recognize a submissive role for women in marriage.

4. Answers will vary.

5. Joining Bible studies is a good way to grow spiritually. Couples can join an in-home study. Men and women can join separate studies at church. And it's always a good idea to do a couple's devotion book or to read the Bible together and pray. It's good to encourage each other to attend Christian conferences. I like to send sermons to my husband. Having Christian friends who present opportunities and encourage spiritual growth is a blessing.

6. It's good to be aware of when you are triggered to lash out so you have an action plan to avoid it. It will vary from person to person and situation to situation.

7. Start with prayer. God can soften hearts. Small encouragements and positive reinforcements go a long way. Praise your husband for going to church. Be sure to thank him for doing a devotion. Ask if you can thank God for food before a meal.

8. Every marriage has seasons, and no marriage is perfect. When you have a godly, trustworthy friend, it is good to ask for prayers without demeaning your husband; you are being honest about your concern for his spiritual condition.

9. We don't know how long we will live. Eternity apart from God is not something to gamble.

Chapter 12

1. Answers will vary.

2. It's good to talk to them with their wives present and to text both them and their wives with the encouragement you give them. If you are a seasoned teacher or leader and have advice and encouragement, be generous in telling them what you have learned.

3. Ask to speak to your pastor or the man who is slighting you about the situation. Maybe the man doesn't even know he is doing it. It's best not to assume it was purposely done. Prayerfully, that's all that will be needed to amend the situation.

4. God tells us to submit and obey in order to make their jobs a joy. There are times it is necessary to speak up because no leader is infallible, but it should be done respectfully, knowing you may be wrong too.

5. Good leaders will work hard for the people they serve. It will be easy to do when they are respected and treated well.

6. News media has become a place that criticizes every aspect of a leader. Social media and even conversations quickly do the same. It's important to be mindful of what we watch and how we talk. We don't need to repeat gossip or take part in criticizing or making fun of those who lead.

7. I struggle to submit to ungodly or immoral people. At times (especially at work) I have no choice as to who is in charge, so I go to work and do the best I can and avoid the gossip and politics. I strive to glorify God regardless of who is calling the shots.

8. The difference is what takes place in your heart, what thoughts you allow to linger in your mind, and what you say about the person to others. Submitting cheerfully glorifies God.

9. Our job is to submit and do our best as God asks of us. God will work out the rest.